handmade
GIFTS UNDER $10

Get ready to save money — and enjoy the excitement of making unique gifts — with Handmade Gifts Under $10! In this all-new addition to the Clever Crafter series, you'll discover inspiring gift ideas for friends, teachers, neighbors, and secret pals. You'll also find ways to spice up special days, including Valentine's Day, Easter, Christmas, wedding anniversaries, and much more. There's even a section of gifts for kids to make or receive. Little ones will feel all grown-up when they make our fun and functional gifts, such as friendship bracelets, a wacky bulletin board, and an autographed pillowcase. Each of the more than 75 crafty projects comes with easy instructions, full-color photos, and a "shopping list" of exactly what you'll need and how much to expect each item to cost. And since every project in this book can be made for less than $10, the only part you'll have to figure out is where to spend all of the money you save!

Anne Childs

LEISURE ARTS, INC.
Little Rock, Arkansas

handmade GIFTS UNDER $10

EDITORIAL STAFF

Vice President and Editor-in-Chief: Anne Van Wagner Childs
Executive Director: Sandra Graham Case
Design Director: Patricia Wallenfang Sowers
Editorial Director: Susan Frantz Wiles
Publications Director: Kristine Anderson Mertes
Creative Art Director: Gloria Bearden
Senior Graphics Art Director: Melinda Stout

DESIGN
Designers: Sandra Spotts Ritchie, Anne Pulliam Stocks,
    Linda Diehl Tiano, and Cherece Athy Watson
Executive Assistants: Debra Smith and Billie Steward
Design Assistant: Melanie Vaughan

TECHNICAL
Managing Editor: Sherry Solida Ford
Senior Technical Writer: Laura Lee Powell
Technical Writers: Jennifer L. Hobbs, Susan McManus Johnson,
    Jennifer S. Potts, and Marley N. Washum
Technical Associate: Linda Luder

EDITORIAL
Managing Editor: Linda L. Trimble
Senior Associate Editor: Stacey Robertson Marshall
Associate Editors: Debby Carr and Janice Teipen Wojcik
Assistant Editor: Terri Leming Davidson

ART
Book/Magazine Graphics Art Director: Diane Thomas
Senior Production Graphics Artist: Michael A. Spigner
Photography Stylists: Beth Carter, Ellen J. Clifton,
    Karen Smart Hall, and Aurora Huston

PROMOTIONS
Managing Editor: Alan Caudle
Associate Editor: Steven M. Cooper
Designer: Dale Rowett
Art Director: Linda Lovette Smart
Publishing Systems Administrator: Cynthia M. Lumpkin
Publishing Systems Assistant: Susan Mary Gray

BUSINESS STAFF

Publisher: Rick Barton
Vice President and General Manager: Thomas L. Carlisle
Vice President, Finance: Tom Siebenmorgen
Vice President, Retail Marketing: Bob Humphrey
Vice President, National Accounts: Pam Stebbins
Retail Marketing Director: Margaret Sweetin
General Merchandise Manager: Cathy Laird

Vice President, Operations: Brian U. Davis
Distribution Director: Rob Thieme
Retail Customer Service Director: Tonie B. Maulding
Retail Customer Service Managers: Carolyn Pruss and
    Wanda Price
Print Production Manager: Fred F. Pruss

Library of Congress Catalog Number 98-67914
International Standard Book Number 1-57486-065-8

Table of Contents

SOMETHING FOR EVERYONE..............6

"F" IS FOR FRIEND..........................8
Friendship Plaque

EASY APPLIQUÉD APRON 10
Sunflower Apron

SEEDS OF FRIENDSHIP 11
Friendship Herb Pot

JUST DUCKY BLANKET 12
Ducky Baby Blanket

CHEERFUL MEMO BOARD 13
Secret Pal Chalkboard

BUSY BEES 14
Bumblebee Wind Chime

LADYBUG LETTERS............................16
Ladybug Note Card Set

WELCOME, NEIGHBOR! 17
New Neighbor Mug and Mat

GARDENER'S DELIGHT 18
Patio Stones

HEARTWARMING WREATH....................19
Friendship Wreath

LULLABY WALL HANGING....................20
Musical Wall Hanging

TEACHER'S PENCIL............................22
Fence Post Pencil

AN APPLE A DAY 23
Grade "A" Teacher Gift

FLOWER POWER................................24
Ribbon Flower Barrettes

FANCY PHOTO KEEPER 25
Fabric-Covered Photo Album

CROCHETED EYEGLASS CASES 26
Crocheted Eyeglass Cases

SOFT-TOUCH HANGERS 28
Crocheted Hangers

JUST FOR BABY 29
Cross-Stitched Baby Sweatshirt

COOKIE TOTE 30
Cross-Stitched Mini Tote

COFFEE LOVER'S CANDLE....................31
Coffee Candle

SUNNY KITCHEN TOWEL 32
Sunflower Dish Towel

LOVELY LAVENDER PILLOW 34
Friendship Lavender Pillow

PRETTY PANSY COASTERS....................35
Pansy Coasters

TEA-TOWEL TOTE 36
Tea-Towel Tote

FLORAL PAGE KEEPERS........................38
Plastic Canvas Bookmarks

Table of Contents

CELEBRATIONS THRU THE YEAR 40

SWEET BOUQUET 42
  Truffle Bouquet
"LOVE-LY" T-SHIRT 44
  Crocheted Heart T-Shirt
SWEETHEART FLOWERPOT 45
  Valentine Flowerpot
VALENTINE SURPRISE 46
  Valentine Door Pocket
ST. PADDY'S WREATH 47
  St. Patrick's Day Wreath
ADORABLE EASTER BUNNY 48
  Sock Bunny
PRETTY EASTER TEE 50
  Easter T-Shirt
"EGG-CEPTIONAL" PLACE MATS 51
  Easter Place Mats
"TEE-RIFIC" GOLF TOWEL 52
  Golf Towel
DADDY'S CADDY 53
  Dad's Armchair Caddy
INVITATION CANDLE 54
  Wedding Candle
WEDDING KEEPSAKE 55
  Wedding Keepsake Box
HERE COMES THE BRIDE! 56
  Bride's Cap
FABULOUS FOURTH ORNAMENTS 57
  Uncle Sam Ornaments
PHOTO PILLOW 58
  Memory Pillow
ANNIVERSARY PHOTO FRAME 59
  Vintage Photo and Frame
TRICK OR TREAT! 60
  Jack-O'-Lantern Candy Bowl

BOO CAT PIN 61
  Black Cat Pin
JACK-O'-LANTERN T-SHIRT 62
  Pumpkin T-Shirt
CANDY CORN PILLOW 63
  Candy Corn Pillow
HAPPY FACE PUMPKINS 64
  Cross-Stitched Pumpkins
BIRTHDAY SNACKS 65
  Moose Treat Container
TURKEY TREATS 66
  Turkey Bowl
AUTUMN ACCESSORIES 67
  Plastic Canvas Autumn Pins
COOL YULE SWEATSHIRT 68
  Christmas Sweatshirt
SWEET ADVENT CALENDAR 69
  Advent Calendar
BROWN BAG ORNAMENTS 70
  Paper Santa Ornaments
GINGERBREAD FRAME 72
  Gingerbread Boy Frame
"BEARY" FUN SWEATSHIRT 73
  Sledding Bear Sweatshirt
FUN FELT SANTA 74
  Santa Shelf-Sitter
SNOWMAN CANDY JAR 75
  Snowman Candy Jar
PET-SHOP ELF 76
  Pet's Elf Costume
ELEGANT STOCKINGS 77
  Tea-Towel Stockings

Table of Contents

FUN STUFF FOR KIDS 80

YOU'RE ON "CANDIED" CAMERA! 82
  Fun Photo Album
BEST FRIENDS 83
  Friendship Bracelet
BUTTON BULLETIN BOARD 84
  Button Bulletin Board
JINGLE BELL SNOWMEN 85
  Snowman Bell Necklaces
ANGEL FACE MIRRORS 86
  Angel Mirrors
BIRTHDAY BEAR 87
  Angel Birthday Bear
BARRETTE BEAUTY 88
  Barrette Beauty
FLOWERS FOR MOM 89
  Flower and Heart Pillow
FRIENDSHIP PILLOWCASE 90
  Friendship Pillowcase

LET'S PRETEND 91
  Dress-Up Kit
PUZZLE PALS 92
  Puzzle Pal Pins
TURTLE TIME 93
  Turtle Pillow
PERKY PUPPETS 94
  Finger Puppets

PATTERNS 96
GENERAL INSTRUCTIONS 123
CREDITS 128

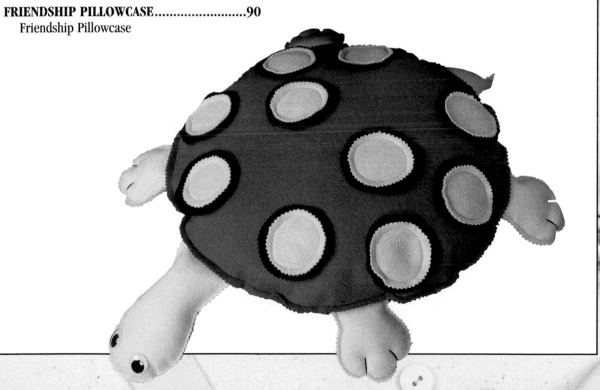

something
FOR EVERYONE

Express sentiments of love and friendship by presenting special people with gifts made by you that are kind to your budget, too! Spice up a friend's kitchen with herbs sprouting from a hand-painted pot, or perk up her porch with a unique bumblebee wind chime. You'll also find ideas for those important times — like a cute blanket or musical wall hanging to welcome a new baby, or a pretty memo board to cheer a secret pal. From best friends to teachers, you'll find something for everyone in this heartwarming collection of crafty projects!

F is for friend — and "S" is for savings! This cute spirit-lifter is a nice way to tell a friend she's special. Economical to make using a few simple materials and easy stitches, this country plaque will warm up any spot in her home.

WHAT TO BUY

$6^5/_8$" x $8^5/_8$" wood-framed chalkboard, $1/_4$ yd. each of tan and red fabric, $3/_8$ yd. of blue fabric, tan and green embroidery floss, and 1 yd. of $5/_8$"w red grosgrain ribbon

THINGS YOU HAVE AT HOME

Paper-backed fusible web, pinking shears, embroidery needle, seven assorted buttons, scraps of assorted fabrics, craft glue, and a hot glue gun

FRIENDSHIP PLAQUE

1. For hearts, cut one $4^1/_2$" x $6^1/_2$" rectangle each from tan and red fabric and two $4^1/_2$" x $6^1/_2$" rectangles from fusible web. For chalkboard cover, cut a 5" x 7" rectangle from blue fabric.

2. Referring to *Fusing Basics* (pg. 123), use pattern and one web rectangle to make heart appliqué from red rectangle. Fuse remaining web rectangle to wrong side of tan rectangle (do not remove paper backing). Center red heart appliqué on right side of tan rectangle; fuse in place. Use pinking shears to cut tan heart $1/_4$" outside edge of red heart; remove paper backing.

3. Center appliqués on blue rectangle; fuse in place.

4. For flowers, sew three buttons onto heart appliqué. Referring to *Embroidery Stitches* (pg. 125), use six strands of green floss to work Lazy Daisy Stitch for leaves and Running Stitch for stems of flowers. Use three strands of tan floss to work Running Stitch for words and a French Knot for dot on "i". Use craft glue to glue blue rectangle to chalkboard.

5. For patchwork on frame, cut various lengths of $3/_4$"w rectangles from fabric scraps; glue onto wood frame of chalkboard, trimming to fit around corners.

6. Hot glue one button to each corner of frame.

7. For streamer, cut a 20" length of ribbon; fold in half. Leaving a $1^1/_2$" loop at top, glue streamer to center back of chalkboard. Cut a 12" length of ribbon; tie into a bow and glue over loop of streamer.

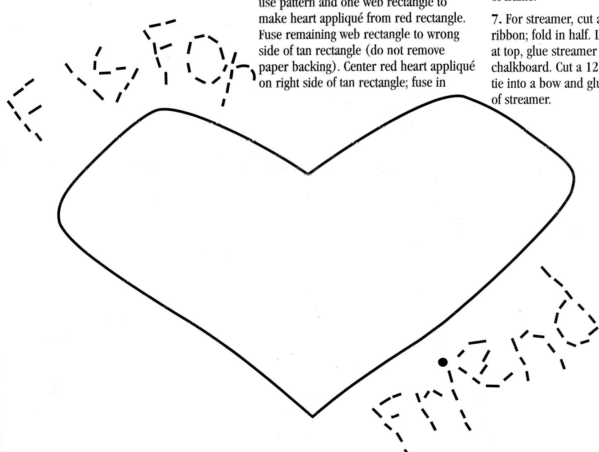

EASY APPLIQUÉD APRON

*H*andmade gifts are great, and giving a friend something she can really use is even better! You'll love how simple and inexpensive this tea-towel apron is to make, and your pal will appreciate how handy it is in the kitchen.

WHAT TO BUY
15" x 26" dish towel; 1/8 yd. each of brown, green, and gold print fabric for appliqués; 1/4 yd. of print fabric for pocket; and 2 1/3 yds. of 3/8"w grosgrain ribbon

THINGS YOU HAVE AT HOME
Paper-backed fusible web, tear-away stabilizer, thread, eleven assorted brown buttons, and clear nylon thread

SUNFLOWER APRON
1. Referring to *Fusing Basics* (pg. 123), use patterns (pg. 96) to make flower petal, flower center, leaf, and stem appliqués.

2. Arrange appliqués on towel, overlapping as necessary; fuse in place. Referring to *Stitched Appliqués* (pg. 123), use clear nylon thread and a narrow zigzag stitch to sew around edges of appliqués.

3. For pocket, cut a 6 1/2" x 12" rectangle from print fabric. Matching right sides and short edges, fold rectangle in half. Using a 1/4" seam allowance and leaving

an opening for turning, stitch along raw edges. Turn pocket right side out and press. Press raw edges of opening 1/4" to inside of pocket. With folded edge of pocket at top, arrange pocket on center of towel, covering 2" of flower stem. Topstitch in place 1/8" from side and bottom edges of pocket.

4. Fold top corners of towel to front of apron. To secure corners, sew a button to center of each folded corner. Sew a button to each top corner of pocket; sew buttons onto flower center.

5. For apron ties, cut one 23" and two 28" lengths of ribbon. Sew one end of 23" ribbon length to each top corner of apron. Sew one end of each 28" ribbon length to each side of apron.

SEEDS OF FRIENDSHIP

UNDER $5!

from one small seed of kindness... friendship grows

Anyone with a sunny windowsill will welcome these herbs sprouting from a cheery hand-painted terra-cotta pot. A leafy green gift like this one will add pizzazz to your pal's home and spice up her cooking, too!

WHAT TO BUY
Three 4$^{1}/_{2}$" dia. clay pots, three 4$^{1}/_{2}$" dia. clay saucers, green paint pen, 4" long garden tools (set of three), tan and black card stock, and three herb plants

THINGS YOU HAVE AT HOME
Tracing paper, transfer paper, stylus, black permanent felt-tip pen, pinking shears, scrap of natural raffia, hole punch, craft glue, and potting soil

FRIENDSHIP HERB POT
1. Trace herb stem and friendship tag patterns (pg. 97) onto tracing paper. Referring to *Making Patterns* (pg. 123), transfer stem pattern continuously around rim of each clay pot.

2. Use paint pen to color leaves and dots on each clay pot and saucer. Use pen to write words and draw designs on each clay pot and saucer.

3. For each tag, use pinking shears to cut a 2" x 4" rectangle from black card stock.

Cut a 1$^{1}/_{2}$" x 3$^{1}/_{2}$" rectangle from tan card stock. Transfer friendship tag pattern to tan rectangle. Use black pen to trace over letters. Center tan rectangle on black rectangle; glue in place. Punch a hole in the top left corner of tag.

4. Cut three 7" lengths of raffia. Thread one raffia length through hole in each tag and tie into a bow to secure around one tool.

5. Plant herbs in clay pots. Insert one tool into soil in each pot.

JUST DUCKY BLANKET

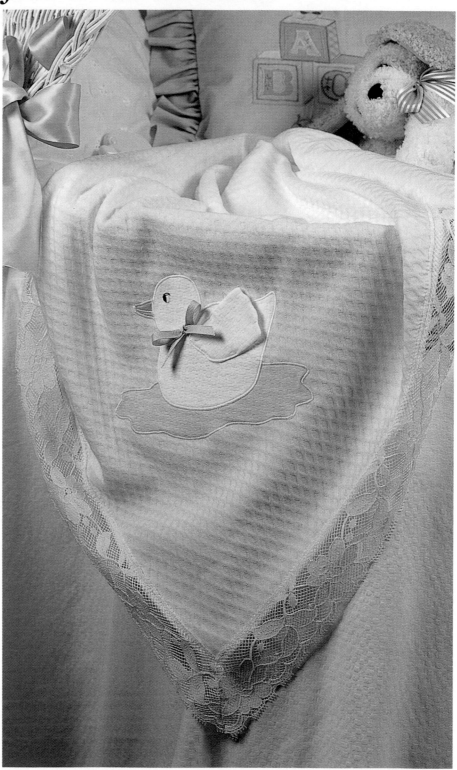

*T*his blanket for baby is "just ducky!" Using a little inexpensive fabric and lace, you can make the snuggly coverlet for a new mother.

WHAT TO BUY
1 yd. of white fabric, $^1/_8$ yd. each of yellow and blue fabric, $4^1/_2$ yds. of 2"w white flat lace, $^1/_3$ yd. of $^1/_4$"w blue ribbon, and black and white embroidery floss

THINGS YOU HAVE AT HOME
Ruler, paper-backed fusible web, tracing paper, fabric marker, scrap of gold fabric, tear-away stabilizer, thread, and an embroidery needle

DUCKY BABY BLANKET
1. For blanket, cut a 36" square from white fabric. Turn edges of blanket $^1/_4$" to wrong side; press.

2. Cut four 41" lengths of lace. Center and pin one piece of lace to each edge of blanket on right side. Beginning and ending stitching $^1/_4$" from turned edges of blanket, sew each length in place.

3. Matching edges, fold one corner of blanket diagonally with right sides together. Use ruler to mark stitching line as shown in Fig. 1 (pg. 39). Backstitching at beginning and end of stitching (Fig. 2, pg. 39), sew along drawn line. Trim seam allowance to $^1/_4$"; press.

(Continued on page 39)

12

*B*righten the day of a secret pal with our cute memo chalkboard that costs less than $7 to make! Hand-painted flowers decorate the border of this handy message-keeper, and a ribbon-tied stick of chalk makes it easy to leave an uplifting message.

WHAT TO BUY

6⅝" x 8⅝" wood-framed chalkboard; white, yellow, light blue, and green acrylic paint; 1 yd. of ⅝"w blue grosgrain ribbon; ⅔ yd. of ¼"w blue grosgrain ribbon; and one box of chalk

THINGS YOU HAVE AT HOME

Paintbrushes, household sponge, pencil with a new eraser, black fine-point felt-tip pen, masking tape, and a hot glue gun

SECRET PAL CHALKBOARD

1. Paint wood frame of chalkboard white; allow to dry.

2. Cut a ¾" square from sponge. Referring to *Painting Basics* (pg. 123), use sponge square and blue paint to stamp checkerboard design on frame; allow to dry.

3. For each flower, dip eraser in yellow paint and stamp three dots close together;

(Continued on page 39)

BUSY BEES

These wind chimes will have folks all abuzz! Turned upside down and painted, clay flowerpots become a "beehive" and a trio of adorable "bees." What a great gift idea for anyone who loves the outdoors!

WHAT TO BUY

6" dia. clay pot, three 1½" dia. clay pots, 4" dia. clay saucer, six 2" x 1" x ³⁄₁₆" wooden primitive heart cutouts, three 1¼" dia. wooden head beads, 8 gauge black craft wire, and yellow and black acrylic paint

THINGS YOU HAVE AT HOME

Craft drill with ¹⁄₁₆" drill bit, paintbrushes, paper towel, white paint, black pen, craft pliers, wire cutters, three 2" long nails, and household cement

BUMBLEBEE WIND CHIME

Allow paint and glue to dry after each application.

1. Drill three evenly spaced holes through rim of clay saucer and two holes ½" apart through center of saucer (Fig. 1). Drill a hole through top center of each head bead.

Fig. 1

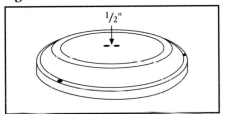

2. For beehive, dip paintbrush in yellow paint; remove excess paint on paper towel (brush should be almost dry to produce good results). Paint outside of large clay pot.

3. For each bee, paint three yellow and two black stripes around small clay pot. Paint head bead black. Using care to not get glue in holes of head or body, glue head to body. Use black and white paint to paint eyes and eyebrows.

4. For wings, use pen to draw detail lines on hearts. Placing points of hearts side by side, glue wings to back of each bee.

5. For each bee hanger, cut a 12" length of wire; use pliers to form a small loop at one end of wire. For antennae, cut a 10" length of wire. Wrap center of wire around head of nail; twist to secure. With nail inside body, insert straight ends of bee hanger and antennae wires through bee. Use pliers to curl ends of antennae wire. Wrap bee hanger wire around pen to curl.

6. For wind chime hanger, cut a 14" length of craft wire; fold in half. Invert clay saucer and thread ends of wire through center holes to inside of saucer; twist ends to secure.

7. Insert ends of bee hanger wires through holes in rim of saucer. Bend ends to outside of saucer (Fig. 2).

Fig. 2

8. Insert wind chime hanger through hole in beehive; twist hanger several times around finger. Bring folded end up through twists to form knot.

LADYBUG LETTERS

Ladybug, ladybug, fly away home — to a perfect spot on our darling stationery! The little red cuties, created from your thumbprints, accent ordinary paper and envelopes. For a charming delivery, line a basket with a red bandanna and glue faux daisies onto the basket and a coordinating pen.

WHAT TO BUY
White note cards with envelopes, red acrylic paint, oblong basket with handles, red bandanna, stem of artificial daisies with water droplets, and a black pen with cap

THINGS YOU HAVE AT HOME
Black permanent fine-point pen, sheet of plain white paper, and a hot glue gun

LADYBUG NOTE CARD SET
1. Use tip of thumb dipped in paint to stamp two "ladybugs" on plain white paper. Stamp ladybugs along bottom and one side of each note card and along bottom of envelope flap; allow to dry.

2. Use pen to draw spots, legs, head, and antennae on each ladybug. Cut ladybugs from plain white paper.

3. To line basket, knot opposite corners of bandanna around handles. Tuck remaining corners into basket.

4. Remove two flowers and four leaves from daisy stem. Glue one flower and two leaves to front of basket. Glue remaining flower and leaves to end of pen cap. Glue one paper ladybug to each flower.

5. Place stationery and pen in basket.

WELCOME, NEIGHBOR!

*N*ew neighbors make great new friends, so welcome them to the block with a thoughtful little gift! A nifty hand-painted mug and matching mat will make anyone feel right at home, especially when their hot cup of tea releases the spicy scent of the mat. And since the cost is less than $6, you can offer a cheerful welcome to every newcomer!

WHAT TO BUY
White 14-oz. ceramic mug, red enamel glass paint, white and red felt pieces, cloves (2-oz. package), ¹/₂ cup rice, and white embroidery floss

THINGS YOU HAVE AT HOME
Tracing paper, tape, and a paintbrush

NEW NEIGHBOR MUG AND MAT
1. Trace flower and flower center patterns (pg. 120) onto tracing paper; cut out. Use flower pattern to cut two flowers from red felt and one flower from white felt. Use flower center pattern to cut two flower centers from white felt and one flower center from red felt.

2. Use paint to freehand "Home Sweet Home" and house on mug; allow to dry.

3. For mat, cut two 5¹/₂" squares from red felt. Arrange flowers and flower centers on one felt square. Use six strands of floss and work Cross Stitches (pg. 125) to sew in place.

4. Matching raw edges, place felt squares together. Leaving an opening for stuffing, use six strands of floss and work Blanket Stitch (pg. 125) around edges of squares.

5. Stuff lightly with cloves and rice; work Blanket Stitch to sew opening closed.

17

GARDENER'S DELIGHT

*D*elight a garden lover with our unique hand-painted patio stones. Using only three colors of paint and inexpensive concrete garden stones, you can create a gift that will bring lasting beauty to a backyard retreat.

WHAT TO BUY
Two 12" dia. concrete garden stones and yellow, copper, and green patio paints

THINGS YOU HAVE AT HOME
Tracing paper, drawing compass, pencil with unused eraser, and paintbrushes

PATIO STONES
1. Trace fleur-de-lis, star, and oak leaf patterns (pg. 96) onto tracing paper; cut out.

2. Use compass to draw 1¹/₄" and 8¹/₂" dia. circle patterns; cut out. Draw around 1¹/₄" pattern on center of one stone. Position and draw around fleur-de-lis pattern four times on stone around drawn circle.

3. Use 8¹/₂" pattern to draw a circle on remaining stone. Draw around star pattern on center of stone. Positioning pattern end-to-end on drawn circle line, draw around oak leaf pattern eight times.

4. Paint designs on stones. Use eraser dipped in yellow paint to paint dots on oak leaf stone. Use copper paint to highlight dots.

5. Use green paint to detail designs.

HEARTWARMING WREATH

Warm the heart of a special pal with this provincial wreath. A cross-stitched message personalizes the project, and a cheery gingham bow accents a bouquet of beautiful spring flowers.

WHAT TO BUY

8" x 10" piece of 14 count white Aida, embroidery floss (see chart and color key, pg. 98), straw wreath with 6" dia. opening, artificial daisies, blue artificial flowers, and 1¹/₈ yds. of 1³/₄"w blue checked wired ribbon

THINGS YOU HAVE AT HOME

Thread, sharp needle, drawing compass, 10" square of poster board, wire cutters, floral wire, and a hot glue gun

FRIENDSHIP WREATH

Before beginning project, refer to Cross Stitch (pg. 124).

1. Use a wide zigzag stitch to sew around raw edges of Aida.

2. Use two strands of floss to work design (chart and color key, pg. 98).

3. For wreath back, use drawing compass to draw a 9¹/₂" dia. circle on poster board; cut out. Center cross stitch design on circle; glue in place. Trim excess Aida to match circle. Center circle on back of wreath; glue in place.

4. Cut several flowers and leaves from stems. Arrange on bottom of wreath; glue in place.

5. Referring to *Multi-Loop Bow* (pg. 124), tie ribbon into a bow. Cut a 12" length of floral wire. Thread wire through knot in bow; twist around bottom of wreath to secure.

6. For wreath hanger, cut a 4" length of floral wire; bend in half, forming a loop. Glue loop ends to back of poster board circle.

LULLABY WALL HANGING

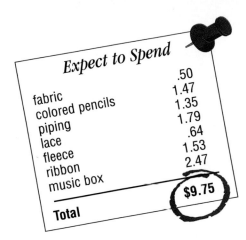

Soothe a little one to sleep with our adorable musical wall hanging. No one will ever guess how little it costs to make! A sleepy moon and a delicate eyelet ruffle make this gift a dream for baby.

WHAT TO BUY

$1/4$ yd. of white fabric, colored pencils (box of 12), maxi piping ($2^1/2$-yd. package), $3/4$ yd. of 2"w gathered eyelet lace, $1/4$ yd. of white fleece, $1^3/4$ yds. of $5/8$"w white ribbon, and a touch AC music box

THINGS YOU HAVE AT HOME

Tracing paper, transfer paper, stylus, drawing compass, poster board, cardboard, polyester fiberfill, thread, and craft glue

MUSICAL WALL HANGING

1. For wall hanging front, cut 9" squares from white fabric and fleece.

2. Trace man-in-the-moon and large and small star patterns (pg. 99) onto tracing paper. Referring to *Making Patterns* (pg. 123), transfer man-in-the-moon pattern to center of fabric square. Cut out star patterns.

3. Use colored pencils to color man-in-the-moon design.

4. Use drawing compass to make 7" dia. circles from poster board and cardboard; cut out. Center fleece square, then fabric square right side up on cardboard circle. Fold excess fabric and fleece to back of circle; glue in place.

5. Cut one 24" length each of piping and lace. Overlapping ends, glue piping around edge of cardboard circle. Turning one end under $1/2$", glue edge of lace to back of circle over piping.

6. Cut one 12", one 18", and two 11" lengths of ribbon. Tie the 18" length into a bow. For hanger, fold the 12" length in half; glue 1" of each end to top back of wall hanging. Glue bow to front of hanger, $3^1/2$" from top of loop. For streamers, glue 1" of one end of each remaining ribbon to bottom back of wall hanging; cut a V-shaped notch in end of each streamer.

7. Glue poster board circle to back of wall hanging.

8. For stars, cut two 4" x 6" rectangles of fabric. Match right sides and raw edges of fabric rectangles. Draw around each pattern on wrong side of one rectangle. Sew around each star along drawn line; cut out. Make a small vertical cut in the middle of one layer of each star; turn right side out and press. Use yellow pencil to color each star. Stuff each star with fiberfill, adding music box in large star. Hand sew openings closed. Glue stars to streamers.

TEACHER'S PENCIL

This giant pencil is a creative way for a teacher to welcome students to the classroom! An ordinary wooden fence post is painted to resemble a classic Number 2 pencil, then natural raffia and a silk bloom are attached.

WHAT TO BUY

1" x 6" x 3 ft. dog-eared fence picket; coral, yellow, silver, and black acrylic paint; natural raffia; one artificial sunflower; and black heavy-gauge craft wire

THINGS YOU HAVE AT HOME

Tracing paper, transfer paper, stylus, ruler, paintbrushes, black permanent marker, hammer, two small nails, wire cutters, and a hot glue gun

FENCE POST PENCIL

Allow paint to dry after applying each color.

1. For pencil lead, draw a line 1$\frac{1}{2}$" from pointed end of fence post. Paint lead of pencil black.

2. For pencil eraser, draw a line around fence picket 3$\frac{1}{2}$" from square end. Draw another line 5$\frac{1}{2}$" from eraser line to make eraser shaft. Paint eraser coral; paint eraser shaft silver.

3. Draw a jagged line 4" from pointed end of fence post. Paint pencil yellow from jagged line to eraser.

4. Spacing $\frac{1}{2}$" apart, use marker to draw three lines on each end of eraser shaft and to write message on pencil.

5. Cut several 45" lengths of raffia; tie into a bow around eraser shaft of pencil. Glue sunflower to knot of bow.

6. For hanger, cut a 5" length of craft wire. Leaving $\frac{1}{4}$" of nails showing, hammer nails into back of pencil 2" from eraser end and 4" apart. Twist one end of hanger wire around each nail.

7. For decorative wire, cut a 24" length of craft wire. Bend three 1" dia. loops along wire; wrap ends of wire around nails to secure.

AN APPLE A DAY

Tickle the fancy of a favorite teacher with a pretty apple look-alike pot filled with gummy worms! Decorated with a cheerful glowworm, the container will have a second life as a clever keeper for classroom necessities or teacher's treats.

WHAT TO BUY

4" dia. clay pot; 4" dia. clay saucer; tan, red, and green acrylic paint; 1¹⁄₈"h wooden spool; stem of artificial leaves; two 5.25-oz. bags of gummy worms; and a 3¹⁄₂" x 9¹⁄₂" cellophane party gift bag

THINGS YOU HAVE AT HOME

Tracing paper, paintbrushes, black acrylic paint, black medium-point felt-tip marker, string, and a hot glue gun

GRADE "A" TEACHER GIFT

1. Paint pot and saucer red; allow to dry.

2. Trace worm pattern (pg. 98) onto tracing paper; cut out. Draw around pattern on clay pot. Paint worm with tan and green stripes. Paint end of worm black. Use marker to draw face on worm.

3. Paint wooden spool tan; allow to dry. Glue spool to center top of inverted saucer.

4. Remove two leaves from stem; glue to bottom of spool.

5. Place candy in bag. Cut two 15" lengths of string; place lengths together and tie into a bow around bag. Place bag in pot.

23

FLOWER POWER

*N*ow all your friends can show off their "flower power!" These bold hair barrettes are a snap to make and fun to wear — and you can fashion four of them for about $1 each!

WHAT TO BUY
Four 9" lengths of 1½"w wired ribbon, 1⅓ yds. of 1"w green wired ribbon, and four 3" long metal barrettes

THINGS YOU HAVE AT HOME
Scraps of assorted fabrics, tracing paper, drawing compass, thread, four buttons, and a hot glue gun

RIBBON FLOWER BARRETTES
1. For each barrette flower, use one 9" length of ribbon. Hold one end of wire to gather tightly along one edge; twist wire ends together to form circle. Matching right sides, glue edges of ribbon ends together.

2. For leaves, cut two 6" lengths of green ribbon. Holding one end of wire, gather ribbon tightly along one edge; twist wire ends together to secure. Pinch ends together; glue to secure.

3. For flower center, use tracing paper and compass to make a 2" dia. circle pattern. Use pattern to cut a circle from fabric. Turn raw edge of circle ¼" to wrong side. Using a double strand of thread, hand baste along turned edge.

Pull ends of thread to tightly gather circle; knot thread and trim ends. Flatten circle.

4. Arrange leaves, flower, flower center, and button on barrette; glue in place.

FANCY PHOTO KEEPER

Photographs are meant to be shared, and a decorative photo album makes a great gift for your mother, sister, or friend. Anyone will enjoy displaying treasured snapshots in this special book.

WHAT TO BUY
10" x 11$^{3}/_{4}$" photo album, $^{3}/_{4}$ yd. of border fabric with one wide border and one narrow border, $^{1}/_{3}$ yd. of batting, and a flower charm

THINGS YOU HAVE AT HOME
Lightweight cardboard and a hot glue gun

FABRIC-COVERED PHOTO ALBUM

1. Measure width and height of open album; cut a piece of batting the determined measurement. Glue batting to outside of closed album.

2. Cut two 3"w fabric strips the height of the album. Glue one long edge of one fabric strip $^{1}/_{4}$" under each side of binder hardware. Glue remaining edges of fabric strips to album.

3. Positioning wide border design on front of album, place open album batting side down on wrong side of fabric. Draw around album. Cut fabric 2" outside drawn line.

4. Center open album on wrong side of fabric piece. Glue corners of fabric over corners of album. Glue all edges of fabric to inside of album, trimming to fit around hardware.

5. Cutting $^{1}/_{2}$" outside each edge of narrow border, cut a 13$^{1}/_{2}$" length from fabric for album trim. Press each long edge $^{1}/_{2}$" to wrong side. Place trim on album; glue ends to inside of album. Pinching trim to gather slightly, glue charm over trim.

6. To cover inside of album, cut two 9$^{1}/_{2}$" x 11" pieces of cardboard. Cut two fabric pieces 1" larger on all sides than cardboard. Center one cardboard piece on wrong side of each fabric piece. Glue edges of fabric to cardboard. Glue wrong side of one cardboard piece to inside of each side of album.

CROCHETED EYEGLASS CASES

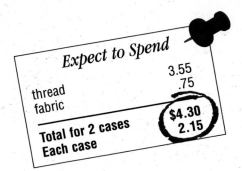

*H*ere's an inexpensive gift idea for all your spec-wearing friends! Using cotton thread and easy stitches, you can crochet these two flower-accented cases in no time.

WHAT TO BUY

One ball each of white and pink bedspread weight cotton thread (size 10) and ¼ yd. of white fabric

THINGS YOU HAVE AT HOME

Size 0 steel crochet hook, paper-backed fusible web, thread, and a sewing needle

CROCHETED EYEGLASS CASES

Before beginning project, refer to Crochet (pg. 126). Front and Back are worked holding two strands of thread together. Use a single strand of thread for finishing Trim.

GAUGE: 17 sc and 16 rows = 2½"

FRONT

Note: Rows 1-19 are worked across length of case.

Ch 37.

Row 1 (Right side): Sc in second ch from hook and in each ch across: 36 sc.

Note: Loop a short piece of thread around first sc worked to mark right side and bottom edge.

Rows 2-19: Ch 1, turn; sc in FLO of each sc across; do not finish off.

Border

Row 1 (Right side): Ch 1, do not turn; sc in end of each row across: 19 sc.

Rows 2-6: Ch 1, turn; sc in FLO of each sc across; do not finish off.

Edging

Ch 1, turn; sc in FLO of each sc across, ch 1; working in end of rows and in free loops of beginning ch, sc in first 6 rows and in next 36 chs, ch 1; sc in end of next 19 rows, ch 1; working in sts across row 19 and in end of rows, sc in first 36 sc and in next 6 rows, ch 1; join with slip st to first sc, finish off: 122 sc.

FLOWER

Rnd 1 (Right side): Ch 2, 6 sc in second ch from hook; do not join.

Rnd 2: Sc in next 6 sc.

Rnd 3: Slip st in next sc, ch 8, ★ slip st in same st and in next sc, ch 8; repeat from ★ 4 times more, slip st in same st; join with slip st to first slip st: 6 loops.

Rnd 4: Ch 1, 12 sc in each loop around; join with slip st to first sc, finish off.

Sew flower to front of case.

BACK

Work same as FRONT.

FINISHING

Make lining as follows: Cut two pieces from fabric, each measuring the size of the Front or Back plus ¼". Turn under ⅜" on each edge of fabric; press. Cut two pieces of fusible web the size of turned fabric pieces. Fuse each fabric piece to wrong side of Front and Back. For added security, sew in place.

Joining Trim

With wrong sides together, Front facing you, and bottom edge to the right, working in ch-1 sps and in both loops of each sc on both pieces, join thread with sc in ch-1 sp at top left corner; working from left to right, ★ work reverse sc in each sc across to next ch-1 sp, work reverse sc in ch-1 sp; repeat from ★ 2 times more; do not finish off.

Top Opening

Working in sps and sts on Front only, work reverse sc in same sp and in each sc across, work reverse sc in same sp as first reverse sc; working in sps and sts on Back only, work reverse sc in same sp as first reverse sc and in each sc across, work reverse sc in last sp; join with slip st to corresponding st on Front, finish off.

SOFT-TOUCH HANGERS

*F*or friends who like a soft touch, our crocheted hangers are the ideal gift. The fun-to-stitch covers fit easily over inexpensive plastic tube hangers, and bows and silk daisies make them perfect additions to a special lady's closet.

WHAT TO BUY
Heavyweight plastic tube hangers (package of three), one skein of blue worsted-weight yarn, one stem artificial daisies, and 3 yds. of 1"w ribbon

THINGS YOU HAVE AT HOME
Size H crochet hook, yarn needle, floral wire, wire cutters, and a hot glue gun

CROCHETED HANGERS
Before beginning project, refer to Crochet (pg. 126).

GAUGE: (sc, ch 1) 3 times = 1¹/₂"

COVER
Ch 145 loosely.

Row 1: Sc in third ch from hook, ★ ch 1, skip next ch, sc in next ch; repeat from ★ across: 72 sps.

Row 2: Ch 2, turn; sc in next ch-1 sp, (ch 1, sc in next sp) across.

Repeat Row 2 until Cover is wide enough to fit loosely over hanger; do not finish off.

Edging: Matching long edges and having first and last rows along outer edge, fold Cover in half over hanger; ch 1, working through both thicknesses in sps along outer edge, sc evenly around; finish off, leaving a long end for sewing.

Thread yarn needle with long end; leaving opening for top of hanger, sew short edges of Cover together.

COLLAR
Ch 7; join with slip st to form a ring.

Rnd 1 (Right side): Ch 1, 10 sc in ring; join with slip st to first sc.

Rnd 2: Ch 3, dc in same st, 2 dc in next sc and in each sc around; join with slip st to top of beginning ch-3: 20 sts.

Rnd 3: Ch 1, sc in same st, ch 1, (sc in next dc, ch 1) around; join with slip st to first sc: 20 ch-1 sps.

Rnds 4 and 5: Slip st in first ch-1 sp, ch 1, sc in same sp, ch 1 (sc in next ch-1 sp, ch 1) around; join with slip st to first sc.

Finish off.

1. Slide Collar over top of hanger and tack in place.

2. Cut a 36" length of ribbon; tie into a double-loop bow. Use wire cutters to cut a 5" length of floral wire. Thread wire through knot in bow; twist ends around top of hanger above Collar.

3. Remove one daisy from stem; glue over knot of bow.

4. Repeat all steps for remaining two hangers.

JUST FOR BABY

*G*ive a little one the gift of snuggly comfort with an adorable cross-stitched sweatshirt. Choose from three lovable designs that take no time to stitch on an inexpensive baby shirt.

WHAT TO BUY
Infant-size white sweatshirt, 5$\frac{1}{2}$" x 6$\frac{1}{2}$" piece of 11 mesh waste canvas, and embroidery floss (see color keys for desired design, pg. 101)

THINGS YOU HAVE AT HOME
Thread, lightweight interfacing, masking tape, sharp needle, tweezers, and a spray bottle filled with water

CROSS-STITCHED BABY SWEATSHIRT

Before beginning project, refer to Cross Stitch (pg. 124).

1. Baste interfacing and waste canvas in place on sweatshirt front.

2. Referring to chart and color key (pg. 101), work design over waste canvas using four strands of floss for Cross Stitch and two strands for Backstitch.

3. Remove waste canvas; trim interfacing close to design.

29

COOKIE TOTE

UNDER $5!

Lift the spirits of a friend who loves sweets with a bag decorated with yummy cookies! An inspirational message is cross stitched on the mini tote bag for a quick and inexpensive gift.

WHAT TO BUY

5½" x 6½" canvas mini tote bag, embroidery floss (see color key, pg. 98), and ¼ yd. of 12 mesh waste canvas

THINGS YOU HAVE AT HOME

Sharp needle, masking tape, thread, tweezers, and a spray bottle filled with water

CROSS-STITCHED MINI TOTE

Before beginning project, refer to Cross Stitch (pg. 124).

1. Baste waste canvas to front of mini tote.

2. Referring to chart and color key (pg. 98), work design over waste canvas using three strands of floss for Cross Stitches and two strands of floss for Backstitches.

3. Remove waste canvas.

COFFEE LOVER'S CANDLE

Expect to Spend

candle	2.99
wax crystals	2.93
coffee beans	1.50
burlap	.75
embroidery floss	.20
ribbon	.50
wooden scoop	.39
Total	**$9.26**

For the coffee lover, create this unique pillar candle for a fraction of the gift-shop price. Dipping an ordinary candle in melted wax and rolling it in coffee beans creates the distinctive look. A burlap bag tied with ribbon and a wooden scoop finishes the offering.

WHAT TO BUY
6"h beige pillar candle, clear wax crystals (12-oz. package), ¼ lb. of whole coffee beans, ¼ yd. of burlap, brown embroidery floss, ¾ yd. of ⅜"w brown grosgrain ribbon, and a small wooden scoop

THINGS YOU HAVE AT HOME
Newspaper, coffee can, saucepan, aluminum foil, tapestry needle and a hot glue gun

COFFEE CANDLE
1. (**Caution**: Do not melt wax in saucepan placed directly on burner.) Cover work area with newspaper. Place enough wax crystals in can to immerse candle. (Remember that melted wax will rise when candle is immersed.) Place can in saucepan; fill saucepan half full with water. Heat water until wax melts.

(Continued on page 39)

31

SUNNY KITCHEN TOWEL

*A*dd a touch of summer to a friend's kitchen with this eye-catching dish towel. You can whip up the sunny crocheted topper in no time, then slip a purchased towel through the plastic canvas bar attached to the back. What an easy and inexpensive way to brighten someone's day!

WHAT TO BUY

One skein each of yellow and brown worsted weight yarn, dish towel, $10^{1}/_{2}$" x $13^{1}/_{2}$" sheet of 7 mesh plastic canvas, and a 6" dia. plastic canvas circle

THINGS YOU HAVE AT HOME

Size H crochet hook and a #16 tapestry needle

SUNFLOWER DISH TOWEL

Before beginning project, refer to Crochet (pg. 126).

GAUGE: Rnds 1 and 2 = $2^{1}/_{2}$"

Rnd 1 (Right side)**:** With brown, ch 4, 11 dc in fourth ch from hook; join with slip st to top of beginning ch-4: 12 sts.

Note: Loop a short piece of yarn around any stitch to mark Rnd 1 as right side.

Rnd 2: Ch 3 (counts as first dc), dc in same st, 2 dc in next dc and in each dc around; join with slip st to first dc, finish off leaving a long end for sewing: 24 dc.

Rnd 3: With right side facing and keeping long end on Rnd 2 to right side of work, join yellow with slip st in any dc; ch 6 loosely, working in back ridges, slip st in second ch from hook, sc in next ch, dc in next 2 chs, sc in last ch (Petal made), ★ slip st in next dc on Rnd 2, ch 6 loosely, working in back ridges, slip st in second ch from hook, sc in next ch, dc in next 2 chs, sc in last ch; repeat from ★ around; join with slip st to first slip st, finish off: 24 Petals.

Rnd 4: With right side facing and working in unworked ch on tip of each Petal, join yellow with sc in any Petal; ch 2, (sc in next Petal, ch 2) around; join with slip st to first sc: 24 sc and 24 ch-2 sps.

Rnd 5: Slip st in first ch-2 sp, ch 1, 3 sc in same sp and in each ch-2 sp around; join with slip st to first sc, finish off, leaving a long end for sewing.

FINISHING
Tie

With yellow, ch 75; with right side facing, join with slip st to any sc on Rnd 5; slip st in next sc, ch 75; finish off.

Assembly

For circular towel bar holder, cut bar from $5^{3}/_{4}$" x 1" piece of plastic canvas (refer to diagram). Place towel bar on plastic circle $1^{3}/_{8}$" from edge, aligning sides. Tack each corner of bar to edge of plastic circle. Thread tapestry needle with yarn end remaining on Rnd 5. With towel bar in back and at bottom edge, place wrong side of Sunflower on plastic circle, centering Tie at top running perpendicular to towel bar. Sew in place through all thicknesses around outer edge of plastic circle. Thread tapestry needle with yarn end remaining on Rnd 2 and sew Rnd 2 to plastic circle, using care not to sew through towel bar.

DIAGRAM

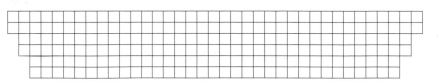

LOVELY LAVENDER PILLOW

The relaxing scent of lavender is the special touch that goes into this delicate friendship pillow. Ideal for the bedroom, this lovely sachet will fill the room with its fragrance.

WHAT TO BUY

$\frac{1}{4}$ yd. of white fabric; $\frac{1}{4}$ yd. of white organza; pink, lavender, and green fabric paint; dried lavender; and $\frac{1}{4}$"w lavender picot-edge ribbon (10-yd. spool)

THINGS YOU HAVE AT HOME

Tracing paper, transfer paper, stylus, thread, white fabric paint, paintbrushes, and polyester fiberfill

FRIENDSHIP LAVENDER PILLOW

Use $\frac{1}{4}$"w seam allowance for all sewing unless otherwise indicated.

1. For pillow, cut two 8" squares from white fabric and one 8" square from organza. For ruffle, cut a $3\frac{1}{2}$" x 60" length of organza, piecing as necessary.

2. Matching wrong sides, pin one white fabric square (pillow back) to organza square. Leaving an opening for adding lavender, sew around edges of squares. Place lavender between layers of fabrics; sew opening closed.

3. Trace "Friends" pattern (pg. 102) onto tracing paper. Referring to *Making Patterns* (pg. 123), transfer pattern to center of remaining white fabric square (pillow front).

4. Paint design using green paint for stems, lavender paint for flowers, and pink paint for word. Use white paint to highlight flowers. Allow paint to dry.

5. Matching right sides, sew short edges of ruffle together to form a circle. Matching wrong sides and raw edges, fold ruffle in half; press. Baste $\frac{1}{4}$" from raw edges of ruffle. Pull thread, drawing gathers to fit around pillow front.

Matching raw edges and adjusting gathers evenly, baste ruffle to pillow front.

6. Matching lavender side of pillow back to right side of pillow front, pin in place. Leaving an opening for stuffing, sew around edges of pillow; turn right side out. Stuff with fiberfill; sew opening closed.

7. Cut four 10" lengths of ribbon; tie each length into a bow. Sew one bow to each corner of pillow.

PRETTY PANSY COASTERS

A basket full of pretty pansy coasters makes a great housewarming gift for a new neighbor. It's easy to stitch the coasters on plastic canvas, so this low-cost offering can be put together in no time.

WHAT TO BUY

One 10¹/₂" x 13¹/₂" sheet of 7 mesh plastic canvas; Needleloft™ plastic canvas yarn: #20 Lemon (two skeins), #39 Eggshell (two skeins), #45 Lilac (one skein), #57 Yellow (one skein), #24 Mint (one skein); 5" dia. basket; and ³/₄ yd. of 1"w wired ribbon

THINGS YOU HAVE AT HOME

Scissors, grease pencil, tissue, and a tapestry needle

PANSY COASTERS

Before beginning project, refer to Plastic Canvas (pg. 126).

Size: 4³/₈" x 5³/₄"

Stitches used: Gobelin Stitch, Backstitch, and Overcast Stitch

1. Cut four 29 x 29 thread squares from plastic canvas. Use grease pencil to outline flower shape. Cut out shape and remove markings with a tissue.

2. Refer to chart and color key (pg. 39) to work required stitches for each coaster.

3. Tie ribbon into a bow around basket. Place coasters in basket.

Yo-yo flowers and buttons adorn this charming tote, which is created from an ordinary tea towel. The old-fashioned basket shape is cut from a lace-trimmed napkin. Whether presented alone or filled with goodies, this useful gift will please a sentimental friend.

WHAT TO BUY

$18^{1}/_{2}$" x 27" tea towel; 12" square white cloth napkin with crocheted edge; and $^{1}/_{8}$ yd. each of pink, yellow, green, and blue fabric

THINGS YOU HAVE AT HOME

Paper-backed fusible web, thread, tracing paper, drawing compass, and three assorted white buttons

TEA-TOWEL TOTE

1. For bag handles, cut a $2^{1}/_{2}$"w strip from each long edge of towel. Remove stitching from hemmed long edge of each strip. Folding handles in half lengthwise, insert raw edge into hem; re-stitch hem and press.

2. Cut an 8" square from one corner of napkin. Matching wrong sides, fold crocheted corner down $3^{1}/_{4}$"; press.

3. Referring to *Fusing Basics* (pg. 123), use basket pattern (page 103) to make appliqué, aligning top of basket pattern with folded edge of 8" square. Use basket handle pattern (pg. 103) to make appliqué from remaining piece of napkin. Center appliqués on one end of towel; fuse in place. Using a narrow zigzag stitch, sew around edges of appliqués.

4. Matching right sides and short edges, fold towel in half. Using a $^{1}/_{4}$" seam allowance, sew sides of bag together.

5. Referring to Fig. 1, match each side seam to fold line at bottom of bag; sew across each corner 1" from point.

Fig. 1

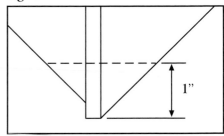

6. Turn bag right side out. Press top edge of bag $^{1}/_{4}$" to wrong side; stitch in place.

7. Use tracing paper and compass to draw a $4^{1}/_{2}$" dia. circle pattern. For each flower, use pattern to cut a circle from fabric. Turn raw edge of each fabric circle $^{1}/_{4}$" to wrong side. Using a double strand of thread, hand baste along turned edge. Pull ends of thread to tightly gather circle; knot thread and trim ends. Flatten circle. Sew a button over center of flower.

8. For each leaf, cut a $2^{1}/_{2}$" square of green fabric; fold square in half. Bring corners of folded edge to center of straight edge; press. Baste along straight edge of leaf; gather and knot threads.

9. Arrange leaves and flowers on front of tote; stitch in place.

10. Spacing ends of tote handles 6" apart, sew ends of handles to inside top of bag.

FLORAL PAGE KEEPERS

*A*ny bookworm will love a marker made especially for her! These lovely plastic canvas page keepers stitch up in a snap for less than $1 each, and they'll be useful reminders of your thoughtfulness.

WHAT TO BUY

10⅝" x 13⅝" sheet of white 10 mesh plastic canvas and embroidery floss (see color key, pg. 104)

THINGS YOU HAVE AT HOME

Tapestry needle and scissors

PLASTIC CANVAS BOOKMARKS

Before beginning project, refer to Plastic Canvas (pg. 126). Backstitches are used for detail and French Knots are worked over completed stitches.

1. For Flower Bookmark, cut a piece of plastic canvas measuring 16 x 72 threads. Refer to chart and color key (pg. 104) and use twelve strands of floss to work design.

2. For LOVE Bookmark, cut a piece of plastic canvas measuring 16 x 68 threads. Refer to chart and color key (pg. 104) and use twelve strands of floss to work design.

UNDER $5!

DUCKY BABY BLANKET
(continued from page 12)

Fig. 1

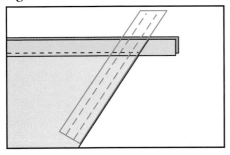

Fig. 2

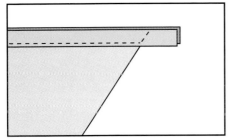

4. Repeat Step 3 to miter lace at each remaining corner of blanket.

5. Referring to *Fusing Basics* (pg. 123), use patterns (pg. 97) to make duck, duck bill, and pond appliqués.

6. Trace wing pattern (pg. 97) onto tracing paper; cut out. Use pattern to cut two wings from yellow fabric. Matching right sides and leaving open between dots, use a 1/4" seam allowance to stitch wings together. Turn right side out. Press open edge 1/4" to inside.

7. Arrange appliqués on one corner of blanket, overlapping as necessary; fuse in place. Follow *Stitched Appliqués* (pg. 123) to Satin Stitch raw edges of appliqués. Topstitching along open edge of wing, sew wing to duck.

8. Use black and white floss to work Satin Stitch (pg. 125) for eyes on duck.

9. Tie ribbon into a bow; sew bow to duck.

SECRET PAL CHALKBOARD
(continued from page 13)

allow to dry. Use green paint to paint stems and leaves between flowers. Use pen to outline flowers and draw detail on stems.

4. Place masking tape 1/4" from inside edge of chalkboard frame. Use yellow paint to paint border on chalkboard; allow to dry.

5. For streamer, cut a 20" length of 5/8"w ribbon; fold in half. Leaving a 1 1/2" loop at top, glue streamer to center back of chalkboard. Cut a 12" length of 5/8"w ribbon; tie into a bow and glue over loop of streamer.

6. For chalk holder, glue one end of 1/4"w ribbon to back of chalkboard. Tie remaining end around one piece of chalk.

7. Write message on chalkboard.

COFFEE CANDLE
(continued from page 31)

2. Sprinkle coffee beans on a 12" square of foil. Holding candle by wick, carefully immerse candle in melted wax; roll in coffee beans. Allow to dry. Repeat twice.

3. For bag, cut a 9 1/2" x 23" rectangle from burlap. To fringe bag, pull several threads from each edge of rectangle. Matching short edges, fold rectangle in half. Use six strands of floss to sew long edges together.

4. Place candle in bag. Tie ribbon into a bow around top of bag.

5. Glue several beans inside wooden scoop; glue scoop to bow.

PANSY COASTERS

COLOR KEY
- lemon
- mint
- eggshell
- lilac
- yellow

celebrations
THRU THE YEAR

Certain days of the year are extra special, so finding the perfect present means a lot. Why not create something yourself that will save you money at the same time! In this collection, we've included plenty of ideas for all kinds of holidays, from Valentine's Day to Christmas. You'll love making a hand-painted sweatshirt to spruce up a friend's Yuletide wardrobe or a handy armchair caddy to wish Dad a happy Father's Day. It's also lots of fun to craft exceptional gifts for other exciting events like weddings, birthdays, and anniversaries. Whenever it's time to celebrate, we've got the gift you're looking for in the pages of this festive section!

SWEET BOUQUET

For someone with a sweet tooth, our scrumptious truffle bouquet is the perfect Valentine's Day gift. Easy to make using paper twist, these candy-filled blossoms look as good as the treats inside taste!

WHAT TO BUY

Box of assorted chocolate candies, one package each of red and green paper twist, two 8" round paper doilies, and 1 yd. of ³⁄₄"w gold wired ribbon

THINGS YOU HAVE AT HOME

Plastic wrap, tracing paper, pencil, heavy-gauge floral wire, wire cutters, and a hot glue gun

TRUFFLE BOUQUET

1. For rose center, wrap one piece of candy in plastic wrap. Cut a 13" length of red paper twist; untwist. Cut a 3" x 13" strip from untwisted paper. Center wrapped candy at end of paper; roll toward opposite end. Twist paper together at top and bottom of rose center.

2. Trace rose petal and rose leaf patterns onto tracing paper; cut out. Use petal pattern to cut six petals from untwisted red paper. Wrap side edges of each petal around pencil to curl (Fig. 1).

Fig. 1

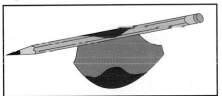

3. Overlapping slightly, glue petals around base of rose; allow to dry.

4. For sepal, cut a 3" square from untwisted green paper twist; cut zigzags along one edge. Glue sepal around base of flower.

5. Use leaf pattern to cut desired number of leaves for flower from untwisted green paper. Glue leaves to base of sepal.

6. For stem, cut 9" lengths of green paper twist and floral wire. Untwisting paper twist stem slightly, work floral wire up through center of stem and into base of flower; glue in place.

7. Repeat Steps 1-6 for remaining five flowers.

8. Cut a 1¹⁄₂" dia. hole in center of each doily. Insert bouquet through holes in doilies.

9. Tie ribbon into a bow around bouquet; cut a V-shaped notch in each ribbon end.

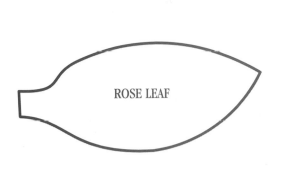

ROSE LEAF

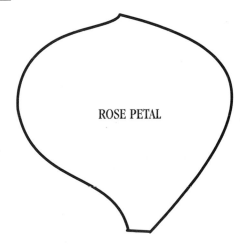

ROSE PETAL

"LOVE-LY" T-SHIRT

*H*ere's a "love-ly" fashion idea for Valentine's Day — or any day. It's a snap to add pretty crocheted hearts to squares of fabric and then use simple stitches to attach them to a T-shirt. It's a low-cost way to sweeten someone's wardrobe!

WHAT TO BUY

Adult-size red T-shirt, size 10 white bedspread cotton thread (400 yds.), ¼ yd. of red print fabric, and four ¾" dia. white buttons

THINGS YOU HAVE AT HOME

Size 8 steel crochet hook and white and red thread

CROCHETED HEART T-SHIRT

Before beginning project, refer to Crochet (pg. 126).

CROCHETED HEART (Make three)
Ch 5; join with slip st to form a ring.

Rnd 1 (Right side): Ch 1, 12 sc in ring; join with slip st to BLO of first sc.

Note: Loop a short piece of thread around any stitch to mark Rnd 1 as right side.

Rnd 2: Ch 1, 2 sc in BLO of same st and each sc around; join with slip st to BLO of first sc: 24 sc.

Rnd 3: Ch 1, sc in BLO of same st, ch 2, skip next sc, ★ sc in BLO of next sc, ch 2,

skip next sc; repeat from ★ around; join with slip st to both loops of first sc: 12 ch-2 sps.

Rnd 4: (Sc, dc, 2 tr, dc, sc) in first ch-2 sp (Petal made) and in each ch-2 sp around; join with slip st to same st as joining: 12 Petals.

Rnd 5: Working behind and between Petals in unworked sc on Rnd 3, ch 8, (tr in next sc, ch 4) around; join with slip st

to fourth ch of beginning ch-8: 12 ch-4 sps.

Rnd 6: Ch 7 (counts as first tr plus ch 3, now and throughout), dc in next ch-4 sp, ch 3, dc in next tr, ch 3, hdc in next ch-4 sp, ch 3, hdc in next tr, ch 3, sc in next ch-4 sp, ch 3, hdc in next tr, ch 3, dc in next ch-4 sp, ch 3, tr in next tr, ch 3, tr in next ch-4 sp,

(Continued on page 78)

SWEETHEART FLOWERPOT

*W*hat a unique way to say you care! Present all your sweethearts with charming but inexpensive hand-painted flowerpots. Fill them with leafy plants that keep on giving long after Valentine's Day is past.

WHAT TO BUY
6" dia. clay pot, 6" dia. clay saucer, white and red acrylic paint, and a ¹/₄" dia. wooden dowel

THINGS YOU HAVE AT HOME
Masking tape, scrap of stencil plastic or a coffee can lid, craft knife, cutting mat, paintbrushes, craft stick, handsaw, and a black permanent medium-tip marker

VALENTINE FLOWERPOT
1. For painting guide, place masking tape ¹/₄" from rim of clay pot and ¹/₄" from rim of clay saucer. Alternating colors, paint squares around pot and saucer above tape; allow to dry.

2. Referring to *Painting Basics* (pg. 123), trace heart pattern (pg. 102) onto stencil plastic. Use craft knife to cut out shape. Using stencil pattern and spacing evenly, paint red hearts around rim of pot.

3. Dip end of craft stick in white paint to paint dots above hearts.

4. Cut a 4" length from dowel. Dip end of dowel in white paint to paint dots below hearts and above squares on rim.

5. Use marker to draw around each heart and to add details between squares and dots.

VALENTINE SURPRISE

UNDER $5!

*W*ant to sneak a treat to your valentine this year? How about a lacy door pocket filled with a sweet surprise! The pocket is a breeze to make, and because each costs less than $4, you can make several for your friends.

WHAT TO BUY
$5^{1}/_{2}$" x 6" heart-shaped Battenberg lace doily, $^{1}/_{4}$"w red picot-edge ribbon (10-yd. spool), red felt piece, $2^{1}/_{2}$" x 6" cellophane bag, and candy hearts

THINGS YOU HAVE AT HOME
Paper or foam cup, aluminum foil, poster board, and craft glue

VALENTINE DOOR POCKET
1. For drying form, cut a section from cup (Fig. 1); place on a 12" square of foil.

Fig. 1

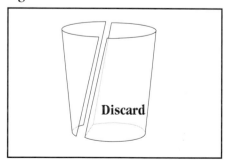

Discard

2. Mix equal parts of glue and water. Saturate doily with glue mixture; squeeze excess glue from doily.

3. Place doily over drying form and press side edges flat; allow to dry.

4. For backing, cut 7" squares from poster board and felt. Aligning edges, glue felt to poster board; allow to dry. Draw around doily on felt side of backing; cut out just inside drawn line.

(Continued on page 78)

ST. PADDY'S WREATH

Pass along the luck o' the Irish with a wreath covered in bright appliquéd shamrocks. Rainbow ribbon and foil-wrapped candy coins add extra charm to this economical gift.

WHAT TO BUY
14" dia. grapevine wreath, poster board, ⅛ yd. each of three green fabrics, 2¼ yds. of 1"w grosgrain ribbon, and gold foil-wrapped coin candies

THINGS YOU HAVE AT HOME
Tracing paper, paper-backed fusible web, and a hot glue gun

ST. PATRICK'S DAY WREATH
1. Cut twenty-five 4½" squares each from poster board, fusible web, and fabrics. Referring to *Fusing Basics* (pg. 123), fuse fabric squares to poster board squares.

2. Trace shamrock pattern (pg. 102) onto tracing paper; cut out. Use pattern to cut 25 shamrocks from fabric-covered squares.

3. Cut five 18" lengths of ribbon. Tie each ribbon length into a bow.

4. Arrange shamrocks, bows, and candy on wreath; glue in place.

ADORABLE EASTER BUNNY

Ordinary athletic socks are the secret to crafting this adorable bunny doll! Dressed in a cute pink dress with lots of bows, the cuddly pal makes a great Easter gift.

WHAT TO BUY

One pair of women's white athletic socks with ribbing, 1⅓ yds. of ¼"w pink grosgrain ribbon, polyester fiberfill, 1½" dia. white pom-poms (package of three), pink felt piece, green and black embroidery floss, and ¼ yd. of pink fabric

THINGS YOU HAVE AT HOME

Thread, embroidery needle, scrap of black felt, fabric glue, tracing paper, and three white buttons

SOCK BUNNY

1. Cut ribbon into four 10" lengths.

2. For body, stuff one sock up to ribbing with fiberfill. For ears, flatten ribbing of sock. Cut along center of ribbing. Matching right sides and long edges, sew ⅛" from long edge of each ear; turn right side out. Stuff ears with fiberfill. Tie one ribbon length 1" from end of each ear and at base of each ear.

3. Cut a 20" length of white thread. To form head, double thread length and wrap around neck of bunny; tie into a knot at back of head. Trim thread ends.

4. For legs, arms, and handkerchief, cut remaining sock as shown in Fig 1.

Fig. 1

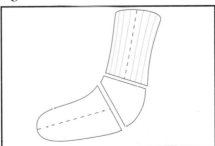

5. For legs, cut ribbing in half lengthwise. Matching right sides and long edges, sew ⅛" from long edge and along one end of each leg, forming a tube; turn right side out. Stuff each leg with fiberfill. Hand sew legs to bottom of body.

6. For arms, cut foot of sock in half lengthwise. Matching right sides and long edges, sew ⅛" from long edge and along one end of each arm, forming a tube; turn right side out. Stuff each arm with fiberfill. Hand sew one arm to each side of body.

7. For face, glue two pom-poms to head. For eyes, cut two ¼" dia. circles from black felt scrap. Use white thread to stitch eyes to head.

8. Referring to *Making Patterns* (pg. 123), trace bunny nose, inner ear, bodice, and pocket patterns (pg. 105) onto tracing paper. Use patterns to cut shapes from pink felt. Glue nose and inner ears in place on bunny.

9. Using six strands of black floss, make long stitches to add details to mouth, hands, and feet.

10. For dress bodice, use ⅛" seam allowance to sew side seams of bodice to notch under arms; turn right side out. For skirt, cut a 6" x 21" strip of fabric. Matching wrong sides and short edges, use a ¼" seam allowance to sew ends together. For hem, turn bottom of skirt ¼" to wrong side; press. Turn ¼" again; press and sew in place. Baste along remaining edge of skirt; pull threads to gather skirt to fit bodice. With skirt seam at back and matching right sides, pin skirt to bodice; sew in place.

11. Referring to *Embroidery Stitches* (pg. 125), use three strands of green floss and work Running Stitch to sew pocket to skirt. Use Stem Stitch and Lazy Daisy Stitch to sew stems and leaves on bodice. For flowers, sew buttons in place on bodice. Tie remaining ribbon into a bow; glue to center of gathers on dress.

12. For handkerchief, fold remainder of sock into a triangle; tuck into pocket.

PRETTY EASTER TEE

Expect to Spend

T-shirt	3.99
fabric	1.54
embroidery floss	.80
Total	**$6.33**

A little girl will find the prettiest eggs of the hunt on the front of this Easter shirt! Pastel fabric appliqués and simple stitches make this inexpensive project a fashionable addition to the "hoppy" holiday.

WHAT TO BUY
Child-size T-shirt; ¹/₈ yd. each of yellow, pink, and green fabric; and yellow, pink, green, and lavender embroidery floss

THINGS YOU HAVE AT HOME
Paper-backed fusible web, embroidery needle, and a white ³/₈" dia. button

EASTER T-SHIRT
1. For appliqué background, cut 4" x 8" rectangles from fusible web and yellow fabric; fuse together. Do not remove paper backing.

2. Referring to *Fusing Basics* (pg. 123), use patterns (pg. 105) to make one tulip, one tulip stem, and two egg appliqués from pink and green fabrics. Arrange appliqués on rectangle; fuse in place. Remove paper backing from rectangle.

3. Referring to *Embroidery Stitches* (pg. 125), use six strands of green floss to work Blanket Stitch around edges of eggs and leaves. Work green Cross Stitches over stem and yellow Cross Stitches along edges of pink stripe. Use pink floss to work Blanket Stitch around flower petals.

4. Center rectangle on T-shirt front; fuse in place. Use lavender floss to work Blanket Stitch around edges of rectangle and Stem Stitch between appliqués.

5. Use lavender floss to work Cross Stitches around sleeves and neck ribbing.

6. Sew button to tulip center.

50

"EGG-CEPTIONAL" PLACE MATS

You won't have to hunt for "egg-ceptional" table decor with these easy-to-craft place mats! By painting foam mats with simple shapes, you can create a set of four for less than $8.

WHAT TO BUY

Four white foam place mats and yellow, peach, pink, and green paint

THINGS YOU HAVE AT HOME

Tracing paper, transfer paper, stylus, and paintbrushes

EASTER PLACE MATS

1. Referring to *Making Patterns* (pg. 123), trace flower, flower center, leaf, and egg patterns (pg. 107) onto tracing paper. Transfer patterns to each place mat; cut out egg shape.

2. Use peach paint to paint stripe on egg, pink to paint ends of egg and flowers, yellow to paint flower centers, and green to paint leaves. Paint a peach-colored dot between each leaf on ends of egg.

51

"TEE-RIFIC" GOLF TOWEL

Expect to Spend

towel	1.54
fabric	1.48
eyelet kit	1.56
slip-sleeve ring	.99
Total	**$5.57**

Using an ordinary towel and some simple appliqués, you can create a useful gift for Dad! Inexpensive materials add to the value of this fun towel, so it's sure to score a hole-in-one with the budget-conscious.

WHAT TO BUY
17" x 26" white towel; ⅛ yd. each of yellow, blue, green, and red fabric; ½" dia. eyelet kit; and one slip-sleeve ring

THINGS YOU HAVE AT HOME
Paper-backed fusible web, tear-away stabilizer, and clear nylon thread

GOLF TOWEL

1. Referring to *Fusing Basics* (pg. 123), use patterns (pg. 106) to make ball, tee, FORE, and grass appliqués from fabrics.

2. Arrange appliqués on towel, overlapping as necessary; fuse in place.

3. Referring to *Stitched Appliqués* (pg. 123), use clear nylon thread and a narrow zigzag stitch to sew appliqués in place.

4. Fold top end of towel as shown in Fig. 1; sew in place.

Fig. 1

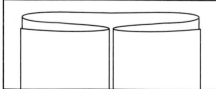

5. Follow kit manufacturer's instructions to attach eyelet to top center of towel.

6. Insert slip-sleeve ring through eyelet.

DADDY'S CADDY

This simple, low-cost project makes the perfect gift for Father's Day! Our fabric caddy fits over the arm of his favorite chair, keeping the television remote control and program guide within comfortable reach.

WHAT TO BUY

¹/₈ yd. of brown print fabric, ¹/₄ yd. of black and white print fabric, ³/₄ yd. of brown plaid fabric, ³/₄ yd. of fusible interfacing, and ¹/₂"w single fold bias tape

THINGS YOU HAVE AT HOME

Black thread

DAD'S ARMCHAIR CADDY

1. For caddy, cut two 8" x 24" rectangles from plaid fabric. For large pocket, cut two 7¹/₂" x 8" pieces from black and white print fabric. For small pocket, cut two 4¹/₂" x 8" pieces from brown print fabric.

2. Follow manufacturer's instructions to fuse interfacing to wrong side of one of each size fabric piece. Matching wrong sides and raw edges, place each pair of fabric pieces together.

3. For pocket bindings, cut two 8" long pieces of bias tape. Follow manufacturer's instructions to bind top edge of each pocket.

4. Placing small pocket on large pocket, stitch a vertical seam through center of small pocket.

5. Position pockets on one end of caddy; sew in place.

6. Use bias tape and follow manufacturer's instructions to bind edges of caddy.

INVITATION CANDLE

Preserve memories of that special day with a handmade wedding candle. The frothy look is simple to create — just whip the melted wax with a whisk! A bow and golden heart add charm to a lace-trimmed invitation.

WHAT TO BUY

9"h white pillar candle, pearl white wax crystals (12-oz. package), 13" length of gathered lace, 13" length of string faux pearls, 15" length of white organza ribbon, and a heart charm

THINGS YOU HAVE AT HOME

Newspaper, coffee can, saucepan, wire whisk, plastic fork, wedding invitation, tracing paper, poster board, thread, and craft glue

WEDDING CANDLE

1. (**Caution**: Do not melt wax in saucepan placed directly on burner.) Cover work area with newspaper. Place can in saucepan; fill saucepan half full with water. Heat water until wax melts; allow to cool slightly.

2. Using wire whisk, whip wax until fluffy. Working quickly, use plastic fork to apply whipped wax to pillar candle. Allow wax to cool completely.

(Continued on page 79)

54

WEDDING KEEPSAKE

*W*edding memories are some of the most treasured ones of a lifetime, so help a bride keep them close to her heart with a lovely keepsake box. Using a few easy-to-find materials, you can create this gift-shop quality present for less than $10.

WHAT TO BUY
10" heart-shaped papier-mâché box, wedding gift wrap, 1 yd. of 1"w white trim, ¼"w white picot-edge ribbon (10-yd. spool), one sprig of white artificial flowers, and two novelty wedding rings

THINGS YOU HAVE AT HOME
Spray adhesive, plastic spoon, wedding invitation, and a hot glue gun

WEDDING KEEPSAKE BOX
1. Remove lid from box. Measure around outside of box; add 1". Measure height of box. Cut a piece of gift wrap the determined measurement. Lightly spray adhesive on wrong side of paper shape. Position paper on box and press in place, smoothing out bubbles or wrinkles.

2. Draw around box lid on wrong side of gift wrap; cut ⅛" outside drawn line. Lightly spray adhesive on wrong side of paper shape. Position and press paper in place on lid. Use back of spoon to smooth paper around edge of lid. Measure around outside of lid; add 1". Measure height of lid; add 1". Cut a strip of gift wrap the determined measurement. Matching edge of strip to top edge of lid, glue strip to sides of lid. Fold excess to inside of lid; glue in place.

3. Measure around outside of box lid; add ½". Cut a length of trim the determined measurement. Overlapping ends, glue trim around box lid.

4. Glue wedding invitation to box lid.

5. Cut a 64" length of ribbon. Referring to *Multi-Loop Bow* (pg. 124), tie ribbon into a bow with four 4" loops and two 12" streamers. Glue flowers to knot of bow. Arrange bow and streamers on box lid; glue in place.

6. Glue rings to wedding invitation.

HERE COMES THE BRIDE!

It's her special time, so let everyone know who's the bride-to-be! Lots of fun for a bridal shower or rehearsal dinner, this cute cap is an inexpensive way to make the event especially memorable.

WHAT TO BUY
White baseball cap, white lace appliqué, $1/2$ yd. of $1/2$"w white lace trim, gold dimensional paint, one sprig of white artificial flowers, $1/3$ yd. of white tulle, and $1/4$"w white satin ribbon (10-yd. spool)

THINGS YOU HAVE AT HOME
Craft glue and a hot glue gun

BRIDE'S CAP

1. Position lace appliqué on front of cap; use craft glue to glue in place. Glue lace trim along stitching on brim; allow to dry.

2. Referring to *Painting Basics* (pg. 123), use paint to embellish lace and flowers and to write "the Bride" on bill of cap; allow to dry.

3. For veil, tie tulle into a bow with long streamers.

4. Cut two 4 ft. lengths of ribbon. Holding both lengths together, tie into a bow. Pull gently on loops of bow to create varied sizes of loops; glue ribbon bow to knot of tulle bow.

5. Glue flowers over knot of ribbon bow.

FABULOUS FOURTH ORNAMENTS

*Y*ou'll love delivering a patriotic message to friends and family with our economical, fun-to-make ornaments cut from brown paper. A simple star-spangled design makes it easy to create the whimsical Uncle Sam. Each one costs about $1.25, so you can pass them out to all your Yankee-Doodle pals!

WHAT TO BUY

Ivory, red, blue, and burnt sienna acrylic paint; 19-gauge black craft wire; and red raffia

THINGS YOU HAVE AT HOME

Brown heavyweight paper bag, tracing paper, transfer paper, stylus, paintbrushes, black acrylic paint, black fine-point felt-tip pen, polyester fiberfill, spray acrylic sealer, an old toothbrush, wire cutters, scraps of assorted fabrics, natural raffia, assorted buttons, and a hot glue gun

UNCLE SAM ORNAMENTS

Allow paint to dry after applying each color.

1. Trace Uncle Sam pattern (pg. 108) onto tracing paper; cut out. Draw around pattern twice on paper bag. Transfer design details to one paper bag shape; cut out shapes.

2. Use white, red, and blue paint to paint design areas of ornament. Paint cheeks

with red paint lightened with a small amount of white paint. Use black paint to paint eyes; use white paint to add details to eyes, cheeks, and nose.

3. Use pen to draw "stitches" on edge of beard and cheeks and to outline mustache.

4. To spatter paint, dip toothbrush bristles into white paint. Blot bristles on paper towel to remove excess paint. Holding toothbrush just above ornament, pull thumb across bristles.

(Continued on page 79)

PHOTO PILLOW

A special family photograph makes this timeless offering truly unique. Transferred onto muslin at a quick-copy shop, the picture is surrounded by exquisite trim, elegant lace, and billowy ruffles. This pillow makes a wonderful gift for National Grandparents Day (the first Sunday in September after Labor Day).

WHAT TO BUY

Transfer of photograph, ¹/₄ yd. of muslin, ¹/₃ yd. of print fabric, 1 yd. of ¹/₄"w braided trim, ¹/₂ yd. of gathered lace trim with ribbon, and polyester fiberfill

THINGS YOU HAVE AT HOME

5" x 7" photograph and thread

MEMORY PILLOW

Use a ¹/₄"w seam allowance for all sewing unless otherwise indicated.

1. Wash, dry, and press all fabrics. Cut a 5¹/₂" x 9¹/₂" rectangle from muslin. From print fabric, cut one 9¹/₂" x 13¹/₂" rectangle for pillow back, two 4¹/₂" x 9¹/₂" rectangles for side panels, and two 5¹/₂" x 20" rectangles for ruffles.

(Continued on page 79)

ANNIVERSARY PHOTO FRAME

*B*ring back romantic memories
of the past for a special couple with
this elegant project. The vintage-look
frame, made using precut mats, is the
ideal way to showcase a photocopy of a
treasured photograph tinted with
watercolors.

WHAT TO BUY
Copy of 5" x 7" photo, 5" x 7" gold mat,
8" x 10" white mat, one tray of
watercolors, 2 yds. of ¼"w trim, ¼"w
ccru ribbon (10-yd. spool), four gold
heart charms, gold acrylic paint, and a
stem of artificial leaves

THINGS YOU HAVE AT HOME
Cardboard, spray adhesive, paintbrush,
and a hot glue gun

VINTAGE PHOTO AND FRAME
*We recommend practice painting on an
extra copy of photo. Avoid more than
one coat of paint on a single area as it
will weaken and curl the paper.*

1. Make a copy of desired black and
white photo.

2. Cut a 5" x 7" piece of cardboard. Use
spray adhesive to glue cardboard piece to
back of copied photo.

3. Thin desired watercolors with a small
amount of water. Use thinned paint to
lightly tint photo.

4. Glue photo to back of gold mat; glue
gold mat to back of white mat.

5. For frame trim, cut two each of 5", 7",
8", and 10" lengths of trim. Cut four 2½"
lengths of trim. Glue one 2½" length of
trim from outside corner to inside corner
of each corner of white mat. Glue

remaining trim to outside and inside
edges of mat. Cut a 40" length of ribbon.
Tie ribbon into a bow 6" from one end.
Glue bow and ribbon streamers around
frame. Glue charms on frame.

6. Remove six leaves from stem. Use gold
paint to lightly paint each leaf; glue leaves
to frame.

7. For hanger, cut an 8" length of ribbon;
fold in half, forming a loop. Glue ends of
loop to back of frame.

Expect to Spend	
bowl	1.69
paint	5.97
chenille stems	.50
craft foam	.79
Total	**$8.95**

*Y*ou can make a festive container to hold Halloween treats for less than $10! Just paint a grinning pumpkin face on a simple glass fish bowl, add craft-foam leaves, and fill it with goodies. The trick-or-treaters will be standing in line!

WHAT TO BUY

6"w hexagonal fish bowl; white, orange, and black enamel glass paint; two green chenille stems; and one sheet of green craft foam

THINGS YOU HAVE AT HOME

Tracing paper, tape, paintbrushes, pencil, craft knife, and craft glue

JACK-O'-LANTERN CANDY BOWL

1. Trace pumpkin leaf and face patterns (pg. 110) onto tracing paper. Cut out leaf pattern. Tape face pattern to inside of bowl.

2. Painting on outside of bowl, paint face orange and eyes and mouth white; allow to dry.

3. Use black paint to outline eyes and mouth, add pupils to eyes, and detail lines to teeth and pumpkin sections; allow to dry.

4. Leaving ends free, twist chenille stems together 3" from one end. Wrap stems around rim of bowl; twist remaining ends together to secure. Wrap each end around pencil to curl.

5. Draw around leaf pattern twice on craft foam. Using craft knife, cut out leaves. Glue leaves to stems.

Boo Cat Pin

UNDER $5!

Need a quick, easy, and economical gift idea for your co-workers or classmates? Here's just the thing — feline Halloween fashion pins! You can craft lots of "spook-tacular" pins for about $6.

WHAT TO BUY

One sheet of black craft foam, one sheet of orange card stock, black bump chenille stems (25-pack), straight black chenille stems (25-pack), ³⁄₈" heart-shaped acrylic jewels, white and orange dimensional paint, and pin backs (4-pack)

THINGS YOU HAVE AT HOME

Decorative-edge craft scissors, craft glue, black medium-point marker, craft knife, and a hot glue gun

BLACK CAT PIN

1. For each card, use craft scissors to cut a 4¹⁄₄" x 5¹⁄₄" rectangle from craft foam and a 4" x 5" rectangle from card stock. Center card stock on craft foam; use craft glue to glue in place. Use marker to write "BOO!" at top of card. Use craft knife to make a ³⁄₄" long horizontal cut slightly left of center of card.

2. For each cat body, bend bump chenille stem as shown in Fig 1. For legs, cut one straight chenille stem in half. Thread one piece through each loop in body; twist to secure. For feet, form ends of legs into loops.

Fig. 1

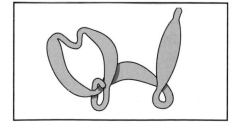

3. Trace cat face pattern (pg. 106) onto tracing paper; cut out. Draw around pattern on craft foam; cut out.

4. Hot glue two jewels on face for eyes.

5. Use white and orange paint to draw nose and mouth on face; allow to dry. Glue face onto cat body.

6. Glue pin back to back of cat; push pin back through opening in card.

JACK-O'-LANTERN T-SHIRT

Expect to Spend

T-shirt	6.46
felt	.40
bias tape	1.45
elastic	.90
embroidery floss	.20
Total	**$9.41**

*G*et ready to be spooked by this festive jack-o'-lantern tee! Decorated with appliqués and simple embroidery stitches, this Halloween top makes a fun gift for a "spirited" time of year.

WHAT TO BUY
Adult-size T-shirt, green and black felt pieces, orange double-fold bias tape, ¹/₄"w elastic, and black embroidery floss

THINGS YOU HAVE AT HOME
Tracing paper, ruler, straight pins, thread, and an embroidery needle

PUMPKIN T-SHIRT
Refer to Embroidery Stitches (pg. 125) and use three strands of floss for all embroidery.

1. Trace eye, nose, mouth, and leaf patterns (pgs. 110 and 111) onto tracing paper. Use patterns to cut pieces from felt.

2. Turn shirt wrong side out and lay flat. Use ruler to draw a line around shirt 6" from hem.

3. For casing, measure around shirt at line; add 1". Cut a length of bias tape the determined measurement. Press each end ¹/₂" to wrong side. Matching pressed ends at one side seam and aligning one edge of bias tape with drawn line, pin tape in place. Using a zigzag stitch, topstitch long edges in place.

4. Arrange eyes, nose, and mouth on shirt front; pin in place. Work Blanket Stitch around each piece.

5. Work Running Stitch along each long edge of leaves. Overlapping slightly, arrange leaves on left shoulder; pin in place.

6. Whipstitch leaves to neckline; continue working Whipstitch around neckline seam, sleeves, and hem.

7. Cut a length of elastic 6" shorter than casing. Insert elastic into casing; overlap ends and stitch together. Adjust gathers evenly.

CANDY CORN PILLOW

Your friends will be delighted with this "sweet" reminder to enjoy our most bewitching holiday. You can whip up cushy comfort at an appealing price — create a candy corn cushion for a spellbinding buddy for about $3!

WHAT TO BUY
Two pieces each of white, yellow, and orange felt; black embroidery floss; and polyester fiberfill

THINGS YOU HAVE AT HOME
Tracing paper, fabric marking pencil, and an embroidery needle

CANDY CORN PILLOW

Use ¹/₄"w seam allowance for all sewing unless otherwise indicated.

1. Referring to *Making Patterns* (pg. 123), trace candy corn patterns (pg. 109) onto tracing paper. Use patterns to cut two candy corn tops from white, two candy corn middles from orange, and two candy corn bottoms from yellow felt.

2. For each side of pillow, sew one top, one middle, and one bottom piece together.

3. Using fabric marking pencil, write "Happy Halloween" on pillow front. Use six strands of black floss and long stitches to stitch words on pillow front.

4. Matching wrong sides, place pillow front and back together. Leaving an opening for stuffing, use six strands of floss and Blanket Stitch (pg. 125) to sew front and back together. Stuff pillow with fiberfill; sew opening closed.

HAPPY FACE PUMPKINS

*G*houls and goblins will take a back seat to the perky pumpkins on this T-shirt! Embellished with jaunty cross-stitched jack-o'-lanterns, this holiday wearable will be the hit of the Halloween carnival.

WHAT TO BUY
Child-size T-shirt, embroidery floss (see color key, pg. 112), and $1/8$ yd. of 8.5 mesh waste canvas

THINGS YOU HAVE AT HOME
Lightweight interfacing, embroidery needle, masking tape, thread, tweezers, and a spray bottle filled with water

CROSS-STITCHED PUMPKINS
Refer to Cross Stitch (pg. 124) for all Cross Stitching.

1. Baste waste canvas and interfacing to center of T-shirt front.

2. Referring to chart and color key (pg. 112), work design over waste canvas using six strands of floss for Cross Stitches and two strands of floss for Backstitches.

3. Remove waste canvas.

BIRTHDAY SNACKS

For a snackin' good time, give the birthday boy a supply of nifty nibbles in a clever container designed to carry his spirit to the rugged North Woods. When the goodies are gone, the felt-trimmed pot can be used as a handy holder for candy or more super snacks!

WHAT TO BUY
4" dia. clay pot, green acrylic paint, tan and red felt pieces, black embroidery floss, one sheet each of green and tan card stock, $3^1/_2$" x $9^1/_2$" cellophane party gift bag, and a 1 lb. can of mixed nuts

THINGS YOU HAVE AT HOME
Tracing paper, paintbrush, embroidery needle, raffia, black pen, hole punch, and craft glue

MOOSE TREAT CONTAINER
1. Beginning $1/_4$" from top of rim, paint outside of clay pot; allow to dry.

2. Trace moose pattern (pg. 104) onto tracing paper. Use pattern to cut moose from tan felt.

3. Cut a 1" x $14^1/_2$" strip of red felt. use six strands of floss and work Blanket Stitch (pg. 125) along long edges of felt strip. Glue strip around rim of pot.

4. For tag, cut a 2" x $3^1/_4$" rectangle from green card stock and a $1^3/_4$ x $2^7/_8$" rectangle from tan card stock. Use pen to write message in center and to draw "blanket stitches" on tan tag. Center tan tag on green tag; glue in place. Punch a hole in top left corner of tag.

5. Pour nuts into cellophane bag. Cut several 20" lengths of raffia; tie into a bow around top of bag. Cut a 5" length of raffia; thread through hole in tag. Tie tag on raffia bow.

TURKEY TREATS

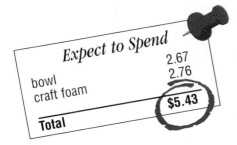
Get ready to "gobble" up the compliments with this turkey treat bowl. Our Tom Turkey was crafted in minutes with just a few colorful pieces of craft foam attached to an ordinary fish bowl. It's perfect for folks who just can't wait for dinner!

WHAT TO BUY

6"w hexagonal fish bowl and orange, red, brown, and black craft foam

THINGS YOU HAVE AT HOME

Tracing paper, craft knife, cutting mat, 1/8" dia. hole punch, craft glue, black permanent fine-point pen, and household cement

TURKEY BOWL

1. Trace turkey patterns (pg. 113) onto tracing paper; cut out. Draw around tail, wing, and beak patterns on orange craft foam, feathers and wattle patterns on red craft foam, turkey body and buckle patterns on brown craft foam, and foot, bow tie, and hat patterns on black craft foam. Use craft knife to cut out shapes. For eyes, punch two holes from black craft foam.

2. Arrange turkey pieces on a flat surface and glue together; allow to dry.

3. Use pen to draw feather lines on turkey body.

4. Glue turkey to bowl using household cement.

AUTUMN ACCESSORIES

UNDER $5!

*S*hare the vibrant colors of fall with these super-inexpensive fashion pins. In just minutes, you can stitch the harvesttime designs on plastic canvas and then attach fasteners to the backs to make fun Thanksgiving accessories.

WHAT TO BUY
Embroidery floss (see color key, pg. 112), 8" x 11" sheet of 14 mesh plastic canvas, five pin backs, and 5mm wiggle eyes

THINGS YOU HAVE AT HOME
Scissors, #24 tapestry needle, clear nylon thread, and craft glue

PLASTIC CANVAS AUTUMN PINS
Before beginning project, refer to Plastic Canvas (pg. 126).

LEAVES (Make four)
1. For each leaf, use six strands of floss to work design (chart and color key, pg. 112) using Overcast Stitch and Tent Stitch.

2. Using long stitches, stitch veins in leaves using three strands of brown floss.

3. Glue one pin back to wrong side of each leaf.

TURKEY
1. Use six strands of floss to work turkey design (chart and color key, pg. 112) using Cross Stitch, Overcast Stitch, Tent Stitch, and Turkey Loop Stitch.

2. Use nylon thread to tack beak to turkey body between *'s. Twist Turkey Loop Stitch to form turkey wattle. Glue wattle and eyes to turkey body. Glue remaining turkey pieces together.

3. Glue pin back to wrong side of turkey.

COOL YULE SWEATSHIRT

*H*ere's wishing someone special a cool Yule! The look is created by outlining the designs with dots of dimensional paint. This festive sweatshirt is sure to make a fashion statement throughout the holiday season.

WHAT TO BUY
Adult-size sweatshirt and white and red dimensional paint

THINGS YOU HAVE AT HOME
Typing paper, straight pins, a T-shirt form or plastic-covered cardboard, and a white fabric marking pencil

CHRISTMAS SWEATSHIRT

1. Wash and dry sweatshirt without using fabric softener; press.

2. Trace horse, tree, gingerbread man, and three star patterns (pg. 114) onto typing paper; cut out. Arrange patterns on sweatshirt front; pin in place.

3. Center T-shirt form inside sweatshirt under patterns. Use marking pencil to draw around each pattern; remove patterns.

4. Referring to *Painting Basics* (pg. 123), use white paint and hold tip of paint bottle just above fabric. Squeeze small dots of paint onto shirt along drawn lines. Gradually spacing dots farther apart, repeat with two more outlines of dots. Add outermost dots at random. Use red paint to draw heart on gingerbread man, dots on tree, and saddle on horse.

5. To launder shirt, turn shirt inside out. Using liquid fabric softener to keep paint soft, hand wash or machine wash on gentle cycle in cold water; allow to air dry. Iron on wrong side only, avoiding design area.

68

SWEET ADVENT CALENDAR

How many days until Santa arrives? This Advent calendar will answer the often-asked Christmas question with candy pieces! In just a few easy steps, you can fashion a fun, inexpensive holiday calendar for each child on your block.

WHAT TO BUY
¹/₃ yd. of quilted fabric, ¹/₄ yd. of green fabric, red yarn, ³/₄"w fusible web tape, and wrapped peppermint candies

THINGS YOU HAVE AT HOME
Scraps of assorted fabrics for appliqués, paper-backed fusible web, a black permanent medium-tip marker, and thread

ADVENT CALENDAR

1. For calendar, cut a 12" x 25¹/₂" rectangle from quilted fabric.

2. Referring to *Fusing Basics* (pg. 123), use patterns (pg. 115) to make star, letters, oval frame, tree, and Santa appliqués from fabric scraps. Arrange appliqués on top half of calendar; fuse in place.

3. Use marker to draw details on Santa, treetop, and stars.

4. For binding, cut a 3" x 90" strip of plaid fabric, piecing as necessary. Press one end ¹/₄" to wrong side. Matching wrong sides, press strip in half lengthwise; unfold. Press long edges to center; refold strip.

5. To attach binding, unfold one long edge. Matching right sides and raw edges, pin binding to calendar edges. Stitching along pressed crease closest to raw edge and mitering corners, sew binding to calendar front until ends of binding overlap ¹/₂"; trim excess binding. Fold binding to back of calendar; blindstitch in place.

6. Cut twenty-four 11" lengths of yarn. Stitch center of each yarn length in place on front of calendar. Tie ends of each yarn length into a bow around one candy piece.

BROWN BAG ORNAMENTS

*M*ake good use of the paper grocery bags that fill up your drawers and cupboards — make these festive ornaments for Christmas! By simply adding a few crafty accents to paper bag cutouts, you can create economical gifts for everyone on your list.

WHAT TO BUY

$1/2$" dia. wooden button; flesh, green, red and burnt sienna acrylic paint; cinnamon stick; green raffia; 19-gauge black craft wire; and a 1" x $3/16$" wooden star

THINGS YOU HAVE AT HOME

Tracing paper, brown heavyweight paper bag, decorative-edge craft scissors, transfer paper, stylus, white and black acrylic paint, paintbrushes, black fine-point felt-tip pen, spray acrylic sealer, scrap of white fabric, assorted scraps of fabrics, assorted buttons, polyester fiberfill, wire cutters, and a hot glue gun

PAPER SANTA ORNAMENTS

Allow paint to dry after applying each color.

1. Trace Paper Santa pattern (pg. 116) onto tracing paper; cut out. For each ornament, draw around pattern twice on paper bag. Use craft scissors to cut out shapes. Referring to *Making Patterns* (pg. 123), transfer detail lines of face to one shape (front).

2. Beginning $1/4$" from edge of transferred shape (front), paint coat red, face flesh, and beard and eyebrows white. Paint cheeks with red paint lightened with a small amount of white paint. Dip handle end of paintbrush in black paint for eyes and in white paint for dots on coat. Highlight eyes and cheeks with white paint. Use pen to draw "stitches" around design.

3. Referring to *Painting Tips* (pg. 123), spray ornament with a light coat of acrylic sealer; allow to dry. For antique effect, thin burnt sienna paint with water; apply to ornament using light brush strokes. Use burnt sienna paint to paint wooden star.

4. For mustache, tear seven $1/4$" x 1" strips of white fabric. Lightly brush burnt sienna paint on each strip. Glue ends of strips together below cheeks.

5. For nose, glue wooden button to face above mustache.

6. For patches, cut three $3/4$" squares from fabric scraps. Glue to front of Santa. Glue buttons near patches.

7. Leaving an opening for stuffing at top, glue front and back of ornament together. Stuff lightly with fiberfill; glue opening closed.

8. For hanger, cut a 24" length of wire. Shape center of wire into a heart; twist wire at bottom of heart. Bend remaining wire to form a semicircle. Insert 1" of wire ends through top of ornament; twist wire together to secure.

9. Cut several 18" lengths of green raffia; tie into a bow around bottom of wire heart. Glue a button over knot of bow.

10. For bows on cinnamon stick, cut five $1/2$" x 2" strips of fabric; tie a knot in center of each strip. Glue strips to cinnamon stick. Glue wooden star to top of cinnamon stick; glue cinnamon stick to ornament front.

GINGERBREAD FRAME

Rosy cheeks and rickrack make great embellishments for this festive fabric gingerbread frame. Friends and family will love seeing a favorite face peeking through the opening in the charming character's tummy!

WHAT TO BUY

8" x 10" x ¼" sheet of foam core board, ¼ yd. each of brown check fabric and fleece, and white baby rickrack (2½-yd. package)

THINGS YOU HAVE AT HOME

Tracing paper, poster board, craft knife, black permanent medium-point pen, scrap of pink fabric, scrap of ribbon, photo, and a hot glue gun

GINGERBREAD BOY FRAME

1. Trace gingerbread boy (including heart opening) pattern (pg. 117) onto tracing paper; cut out. Draw around pattern on foam core board, poster board, and fleece. Using craft knife, cut out shapes. Cut heart openings from foam core board and fleece shapes. Glue fleece shape to foam core board shape.

2. Cut a 9" square from brown fabric. Draw around pattern on wrong side of fabric square. Cutting ¾" outside drawn line of gingerbread boy pattern, cut shape from fabric square. Cutting ¾" inside drawn line of heart, cut out heart

opening. Make clips in heart opening to within ⅛" of drawn line of heart.

3. Center fabric shape over fleece on foam core board shape; glue in place. Clipping as necessary, turn all raw edges to wrong side of foam core board; glue in place.

4. Use pen to draw eyes and mouth on gingerbread boy. For cheeks, cut two ½" dia. circles from pink fabric; glue to face of gingerbread boy.

5. Cut one 11" and one 33" length of rickrack. Trimming ends as necessary, glue 33" length around edge of frame. Glue 11" length around edge of heart opening.

6. Center photo behind frame opening; glue in place. Glue poster board shape to back of frame.

7. For frame stand, cut two 1" x 4¼" strips of poster board; glue strips together. Fold one end of stand ½" to one side; glue folded end to center back of frame. Cut a 2½" length of ribbon; glue ½" of one end of ribbon to underside of stand. Glue ½" of opposite end to frame (Fig. 1).

Fig. 1

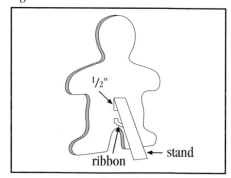

½"

ribbon   stand

"Beary" Fun Sweatshirt

A snow-loving kid will get a kick out of this "beary" cute sweatshirt. The sledding bear is a cinch to appliqué using felt and embroidery floss, and the whole project costs less than $7 to make!

WHAT TO BUY

Child-size white sweatshirt; tan, green, and brown felt pieces; and black embroidery floss

THINGS YOU HAVE AT HOME

Tracing paper, paper-backed fusible web, scrap of red fabric, straight pins, an embroidery needle, black button, and a scrap of fabric for scarf

SLEDDING BEAR SWEATSHIRT

1. Trace bear, muzzle, and sled patterns (pg. 118) onto tracing paper; cut out. Use patterns to cut bear from tan felt, muzzle from brown felt, and sled from green felt.

2. Referring to *Fusing Basics* (pg. 123), use ear and paw patterns (pg. 118) to make appliqués from red fabric scrap. Arrange appliqués on bear; fuse in place.

3. Arrange bear and sled on sweatshirt front; pin in place.

4. Referring to *Embroidery Stitches* (pg. 125), use six strands of floss to work Satin Stitch for nose and Stem Stitch around ears and paws, for arm and leg lines, and for mouth. Work French Knots

for eyes. Use Blanket Stitch to stitch edges of appliqués to sweatshirt.

5. For sled rope, cut a 13" length of floss; thread through button. Tack button to sled, and rope under bear's hands.

6. For scarf, tear a 1" x 10" strip of fabric. Fold in half; tie a knot 2" from fold. Tack scarf to bear's neck.

73

UNDER $5!

This jolly button-nosed Santa will be the star of any holiday home! Fashioned from felt, the miniature St. Nick assembles quickly with so-easy embroidery stitches and glue. And since the jolly old gent costs less than $3.50 to make, he's a bargain to boot!

WHAT TO BUY
White, flesh, pink, red, purple, and black felt pieces; white and black embroidery floss; and polyester fiberfill

THINGS YOU HAVE AT HOME
Tracing paper, cardboard, embroidery needle, thread, red button, and craft glue

SANTA SHELF-SITTER
1. Trace Santa and base patterns (pg. 119) onto tracing paper; cut out. Use patterns to cut two Santa body pieces from red felt; face from flesh felt; hatband, coat trim, beard, mustache, and base from white felt; two cheeks from pink felt; one belt from black felt; and one star from purple felt. Draw around base pattern on cardboard. Cut out shape slightly inside drawn line.

2. Arrange face, beard, mustache, hatband, and coat trim on one body piece (front); pin in place. Referring to *Embroidery Stitches* (pg. 125), use three strands of black floss to work Blanket Stitch around edges of appliqués and French Knots for eyes. Work Cross Stitches on hat above hatband. For nose, sew button to face.

3. Glue cheeks to face; glue belt and star below beard. Glue felt base to cardboard base.

4. Matching right sides, use a ¼" seam allowance to sew front and back pieces together. Clip curves and turn right side out; stuff firmly with fiberfill.

5. Place base over fiberfill at bottom of body; hand sew in place.

SNOWMAN CANDY JAR

*W*hy not deliver your sweet treats in a handsome snowman candy jar that neighbors will love! An inexpensive doily transforms an ordinary jar into a fun holiday container.

WHAT TO BUY

4" dia. crocheted doily, orange and black felt pieces, ¹/₈ yd. of ³/₈"w red grosgrain ribbon, ¹/₂ yd. of 1"w dotted grosgrain ribbon, and two 6-oz. pkgs. of peppermint candies

THINGS YOU HAVE AT HOME

Tracing paper, drawing compass, scraps of two fabrics, thread, ³/₈" dia. red button, silk holly leaf, two ¹/₂" dia. black buttons, quart-size canning jar with lid and lid rim, and a hot glue gun

SNOWMAN CANDY JAR

1. Trace hat and snowman nose patterns (pg. 116) onto tracing paper; cut out. Using patterns, cut one hat from black felt and one nose from orange felt.

2. For flower on hat, use tracing paper and compass to make a 2" dia. circle pattern. Use pattern to cut a circle from one fabric scrap. Turn raw edge of circle ¹/₄" to wrong side. Using a double strand of thread, hand baste along turned edge. Pull ends of thread to tightly gather circle; knot thread and trim ends. Flatten circle. Glue red button over center of flower.

3. For hatband, glue ³/₈"w ribbon, holly leaf, and flower to hat, trimming ribbon as necessary.

4. Arrange hat, black buttons, and nose on doily; glue in place. Glue snowman to jar. For scarf, knot 1"w ribbon around jar.

(Continued on page 79)

PET-SHOP ELF

*N*eed a little magic around your "workshop" during the holidays? Just dress up your pet in a festive elf hat and collar! Simply cut the pieces from felt and attach ribbons and tiny jingle bells. What a fun way to include your four-legged friends in your merry-making!

WHAT TO BUY
1/2 yd. of green felt, 4mm red silk ribbon (two 3-yd. packages), eleven 12mm jingle bells, holly pick with small leaves, and elastic cord

THINGS YOU HAVE AT HOME
Tracing paper, thread, tapestry needle, and craft glue

PET'S ELF COSTUME
1. Referring to *Making Patterns* (pg. 123), trace collar pattern (pg. 120) onto tracing paper; cut out. Matching fold line of pattern with fold of felt, use pattern to cut collar from felt. Cut along one fold of collar.

2. Sew one jingle bell to each point of collar. Cut eleven 8" lengths of ribbon; tie one length in a bow around each point above bell.

3. Leaving a 6" tail on each end, hand sew ribbon around neck edge of collar.

4. For hat, cut a 12" square from felt. Overlapping 1/2", glue two adjacent edges together, forming a point. Cut a 12" length of elastic; sew ends to edge of hat 4" from each side of glued seam.

5. Remove three holly leaves from pick; glue to point of hat. Sew one jingle bell to center of holly leaves. Tie remaining ribbon length into a bow at point of hat.

ELEGANT STOCKINGS

Expect to Spend

towel	5.50
fabric	.60
doily	1.60
ribbon	.34
Total for 2 stockings	**$8.04**
Each stocking	**4.02**

A special friend will love an elegant tea-towel stocking to fill with little treats! A Battenberg lace cuff adds a fanciful touch to this beautiful holiday accent that costs about $4 to make.

WHAT TO BUY

24" square tea towel, ¹/₄ yd. white fabric, 6" square Battenberg doily, and ¹/₂ yd. of ³/₈"w white ribbon

THINGS YOU HAVE AT HOME

Tracing paper, thread, and two ³/₄" dia. buttons

TEA-TOWEL STOCKINGS

Use ¹/₄"w seam allowance for all sewing unless otherwise indicated.

1. Referring to *Making Patterns* (pg. 123), trace stocking pattern (pg. 121) onto tracing paper; cut out. For each stocking, use pattern to cut two shapes each from fabric and towel.

2. Cut doily in half diagonally. Matching raw edges and right sides, position one doily triangle between stocking front and back; pin in place. Leaving top edges open, sew around stocking. Clip curves as necessary. Turn right side out; press.

3. For stocking trim, cut a 1" x 9¹/₂" strip from towel. Matching right sides and

short edges, sew short edges together, forming a loop. Turn right side out; press seam flat. Matching wrong sides and raw edges, fold trim in half; press. Matching right sides and raw edges, sew trim around top of stocking.

4. Leaving top edges open and 3" open along one side for turning, stitch around stocking lining; clip curves as necessary.

5. Matching right sides and top raw edges, insert stocking into lining; sew around top edge of stocking. Turn right side out; sew opening closed. Turn lining to inside of stocking.

6. For hanger, cut a 9" length of ribbon. Cross ribbon 1" from ends, forming a loop. Sew button and ribbon loop to top of stocking at back seam.

CROCHETED HEART T-SHIRT
(Continued from page 44)

ch 3, dc in next tr, ch 3, dc in next ch-4 sp, ch 3, sc in next tr, ch 3, dc in next ch-4 sp, ch 3, dc in next tr, ch 3, tr in next ch-4 sp, ch 3, tr in next tr, ch 3, dc in next ch-4 sp, ch 3, hdc in next tr, ch 3, sc in next ch-4 sp, ch 3, hdc in next tr, ch 3, hdc in next ch-4 sp, ch 3, dc in next tr, ch 3, dc in last ch-4 sp, ch 3; join with slip st to first tr: 24 ch-3 sps.

Rnd 7: Ch 7, dc in next dc, ch 3, hdc in next dc, ch 3, hdc in next hdc, ch 3, dc in next hdc, ch 3, dc in next sc, ch 3, dc in next hdc, ch 3, dc in next dc, ch 3, (tr, ch 3) twice in next 2 tr, tr in next dc, ch 3, dc in next dc, ch 3, slip st in next sc, ch 3, dc in next dc, ch 3, tr in next dc, ch 3, (tr, ch 3) twice in next 2 tr, dc in next dc, ch 3, dc in next hdc, ch 3, dc in next sc, ch 3, dc in next hdc, ch 3, hdc in next hdc, ch 3, hdc in next dc, ch 3, dc in last dc, ch 3; join with slip st to first tr: 28 ch-3 sps.

Rnd 8: Ch 7, dc in next ch-3 sp, ch 3, dc in next dc, ch 3, (dc in next hdc, ch 3) twice, (dc in next dc, ch 3) 4 times, dc in next tr, ch 3, (dc in next ch-3 sp, ch 3) 3 times, (dc in next tr, ch 3) twice, hdc in next dc, ch 3, slip st in next slip st, ch 3, hdc in next dc, ch 3, (dc in next tr, ch 3) twice, (dc in next ch-3 sp, ch 3) 3 times, dc in next tr, ch 3, (dc in next dc, ch 3) 4 times, (dc in next hdc, ch 3) twice, dc in next dc, ch 3, dc in last ch-3 sp, ch 3; join with slip st to first tr: 32 ch-3 sps.

Rnd 9: Ch 7, dc in next dc, ch 3, (dc in next ch-3 sp, ch 3) 3 times, (dc in next dc, ch 3) 4 times, (dc in next ch-3 sp, ch 3) twice, (dc in next dc, ch 3) 3 times, (dc in next ch-3 sp, ch 3) twice, dc in next dc, ch 3, (dc in next ch-3 sp, ch 3) twice, dc in next hdc, ch 3, slip st in next slip st, ch 3, dc in next hdc, ch 3, (dc in next ch-3 sp, ch 3) twice, dc in next dc, ch 3, (dc in next ch-3 sp, ch 3) twice, (dc in next dc, ch 3) 3 times, (dc in next ch-3 sp, ch 3) twice, (dc in next dc, ch 3) 4 times, (dc in next ch-3 sp, ch 3) 3 times, dc in last dc, ch 3; join with slip st to first tr: 40 ch-3 sps.

Rnd 10: Ch 1, sc in same st, ch 2, slip st in top of sc just made, (2 sc in next ch-3 sp, sc in next dc, ch 2, slip st in top of sc just made) 19 times, 2 sc in each of next 2 ch-3 sps, (sc in next dc, ch 2, slip st in top of sc just made, 2 sc in next ch-3 sp) around; join with slip st to first sc, finish off.

FLOWER (Make three)
Work same as Crocheted Heart for four rounds; finish off.

1. For heart backgrounds, cut three 6" and three 3¹/₂" squares from fabric. Turn edges of each square ¹/₄" to wrong side; press. Arrange squares on T-shirt front; topstitch along edges to secure.

2. Center hearts on large squares and flowers on small squares; use white thread to hand stitch around edges to secure.

3. For sleeve bands, cut two 1³/₄" x 17" strips of fabric. Turn long edges of each strip ¹/₄" to wrong side; press. Turn one end of each strip ¹/₂" to wrong side; press. Arrange one strip around cuff of each sleeve; pin in place. Topstitch along edges of each sleeve band to secure.

4. Sew two buttons 1¹/₂" apart on each sleeve.

VALENTINE DOOR POCKET
(Continued from page 46)

5. Cut an 11" length of ribbon. Glue ribbon ends to top edge on felt side of backing.

6. For pocket, glue flat edges of doily to felt side of backing; allow to dry.

7. Cut two 7" lengths of ribbon; tie each length into a bow. Glue bows to front of pocket.

8. Fill bag with candy. Cut an 8" length of ribbon; tie into a bow around top of bag. Place bag in pocket.

WEDDING CANDLE
(Continued from page 54)

3. Glue invitation to a 6" square of poster board. Trace oval pattern onto tracing paper; cut out. Center pattern over invitation; cut out.

4. Overlapping ends, glue edges of lace to back of poster board oval. With ends at top of invitation, glue pearls around front edge of oval.

5. Tie ribbon into a bow; sew charm to knot of bow. Glue bow to top center of invitation.

6. Glue invitation to front of candle.

UNCLE SAM ORNAMENTS
(Continued from page 57)

5. Spray ornament with a light coat of acrylic sealer; allow to dry. For antique effect, thin burnt sienna paint with water; apply to ornament using light brush strokes.

6. Leaving an opening for stuffing at top, glue front and back of ornament together. Stuff ornament lightly with fiberfill; glue top together.

7. For hanger, cut a 25" length of wire. Curl wire around a pencil. Insert 1" of wire ends through top of ornament; pinch wire together to secure.

8. Cut several 18" lengths of raffia; tie into a bow around top of hanger. For fabric bow, cut a 1" x $3^{1}/_{4}$" strip of fabric. Tie a knot at center of fabric strip; glue to knot of raffia bow. Glue a button over knot of fabric bow.

9. For patches, cut two $3/_{4}$" squares from fabric scraps; glue on bottom of beard. Glue a button over center of patches.

MEMORY PILLOW
(Continued from page 58)

2. Have photograph transferred to center of muslin rectangle at a copy center.

3. Matching right sides and long edges, sew one side panel to each side of photograph rectangle to make pillow top.

4. Cut two $5^{1}/_{2}$" and two $9^{1}/_{2}$" lengths of braided trim. Covering top and bottom edges of photograph, sew $5^{1}/_{2}$" lengths of trim to pillow top. Covering seams, sew $9^{1}/_{2}$" lengths of trim to pillow top.

5. Cut two $9^{1}/_{2}$" lengths of lace. Sew one length $3/_{4}$" from each edge of photo.

6. For each ruffle, match right sides and long edges to fold ruffle fabric in half. Sew across each short end; turn right side out. Baste $1/_{4}$" from long edges. Pull threads to gather ruffle to fit one short edge of pillow top. Matching raw edges, pin one ruffle to each end on right side of pillow top.

7. Matching right sides and leaving an opening for turning, sew pillow top and pillow back together; turn right side out. Stuff with fiberfill; sew opening closed.

SNOWMAN CANDY JAR
(Continued from page 75)

5. Remove jar lid and rim from jar. Place jar lid on wrong side of remaining fabric scrap; draw around lid. Cut out circle; glue to top of lid.

6. Fill jar with candy; replace jar lid and rim.

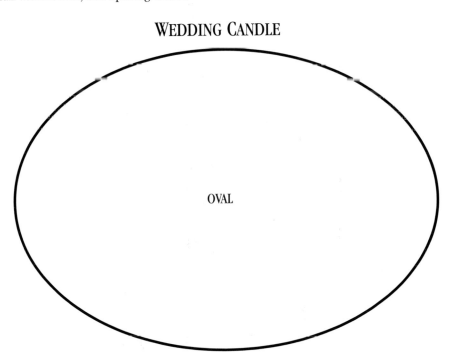

WEDDING CANDLE

OVAL

fun stuff FOR KIDS

Crafting is a great way to provide youngsters with hours of quality entertainment! This extraordinary section is jam-packed with projects that are guaranteed to be fun for children to make or receive — and each one fits a kid-size budget. Young ones will delight in making a colorful button-embellished bulletin board or fun photo album for a friend. A flowered felt pillow makes a cherished Mother's Day gift, and design-your-own pillowcases are creative favors for a slumber party. Whatever the occasion, you're sure to find the perfect present for little folks in this cute collection of clever crafts!

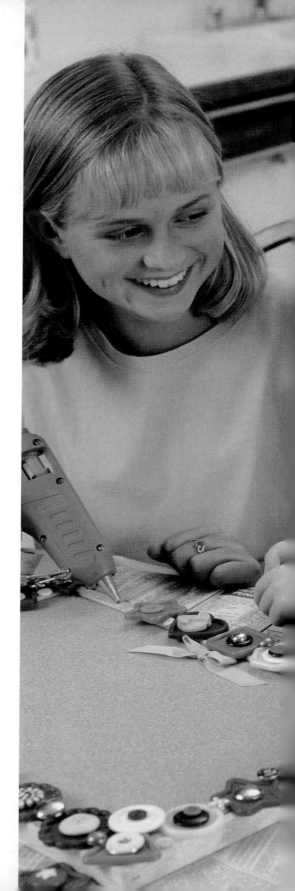

YOU'RE ON "CANDIED" CAMERA!

*S*mile! You're on "candied" camera! A collage of candy wrappers and stickers, accented with bright paint, makes it easy for a young shutterbug to create a one-of-a-kind photo album cover.

WHAT TO BUY
5" x 7" photo album, pink dimensional paint, and ³/₄"h gold alphabet stickers

THINGS YOU HAVE AT HOME
Assorted candy wrappers, denatured alcohol, rubber cement, spray acrylic sealer, decorative-edge craft scissors, corrugated cardboard, black permanent medium-tip marker, and a hot glue gun

FUN PHOTO ALBUM
1. Clean back of candy wrappers with alcohol. Cut wrappers into desired shapes; use rubber cement to glue wrapper shapes to album front. Spray album front with acrylic sealer; allow to dry.

2. Referring to *Painting Basics* (pg. 123), use paint to outline edges of wrappers; allow to dry.

3. Use craft scissors to cut a 1¹/₄" x 4" strip of cardboard. Use stickers to spell out "PHOTOS" on one side of cardboard strip. Use marker to outline each letter. Paint edges of cardboard strip; allow to dry.

4. Glue cardboard strip onto front of photo album.

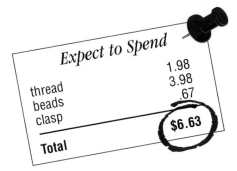
BEST FRIENDS

A gift between friends should be special — that's why an easy-to-make bracelet is the perfect idea for young folks! Inexpensive waxed thread is laced with alphabet beads to spell "best friends," along with colorful accents to add flair.

WHAT TO BUY

Black waxed-linen thread, alphabet beads, solid and striped opaque beads, and a hook and eye clasp

FRIENDSHIP BRACELET

Finished project yields a 7¹/₂" bracelet.

1. Cut a 4¹/₂ ft. length of linen thread. Thread eye clasp onto thread 12" from one end; fold down. Tie an Overhand Knot (Fig. 1) below eye.

Fig. 1

2. Thread a bead onto short end of thread. Work a Buttonhole Knot (Fig. 2) around bead with longer thread length; repeat with four more beads. Knotting between beads, thread alternating alphabet beads and opaque beads until "BEST FRIENDS" has been spelled out, threading a heart bead and two opaque beads between the words. Add five more beads to end of bracelet.

Fig. 2

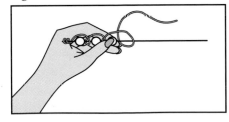

3. Tie hook onto bracelet with remaining 12" length using Overhand Knot.

4. Working toward eye clasp, use remaining longer end of thread to work Buttonhole Knot on opposite sides of beads; tie off to finish.

83

BUTTON BULLETIN BOARD

An assortment of colorful buttons makes this eye-catching project so much fun! An ordinary cork bulletin board is bordered with buttons of all shapes and sizes for a kid-friendly look.

WHAT TO BUY
11" x 17" wood-framed bulletin board, large craft buttons (1/4-lb. bag), and assorted buttons (200-piece bag)

THINGS YOU HAVE AT HOME
Scrap of ribbon and a hot glue gun

BUTTON BULLETIN BOARD

1. Glue buttons onto frame of bulletin board as desired.

2. Tie ribbon into a bow; glue to center top of bulletin board.

JINGLE BELL SNOWMEN

*Y*oungsters can jingle all the way this Christmas when you pass out snowman bell necklaces! These frosty fellows are a cinch to make using painted jingle bells, and you can make lots of "snow" for just a little "dough."

WHAT TO BUY
35mm jingle bells (four 2-packs), white acrylic paint, 1/4" dia. green pom-poms, orange and black craft foam, white wrapped floral wire, and red yarn

THINGS YOU HAVE AT HOME
Paintbrush, 1/8" dia. hole punch, craft glue, and a hot glue gun

SNOWMAN BELL NECKLACES

1. For each snowman, paint bell white; allow to dry.

2. For eyes and mouth, punch seven circles from black foam. For nose, cut a 3/8" long carrot shape from orange foam. Holding bell upside down, glue foam pieces for face to bell; allow to dry.

3. For ear muffs, cut a 2 1/2" length of wire. Bend wire into a half-circle; hot glue one end to each side of bell. Glue one pom-pom over each end of wire.

4. For necklace, cut desired length of yarn; fold in half. Place looped end of yarn under wire. Bring both ends of yarn through the loop and pull to close loop; knot ends together.

ANGEL FACE MIRRORS

Little girls will love crafting these dazzling hand mirrors at a birthday celebration. The cute projects are budget-friendly, too, because each one costs less than $4 to make. Just one look in these mirrors will reveal the faces of angels!

WHAT TO BUY
Three small hand-held mirrors, gold chenille stems (25-pack), six 2" x 4$^{1}/_{2}$" satin puffy wings, 3 yds. of $^{1}/_{8}$"w pink satin ribbon, and nine heart-shaped acrylic jewels

THINGS YOU HAVE AT HOME
Hot glue gun

ANGEL MIRRORS
1. For each halo, form one end of chenille stem into a 2$^{1}/_{2}$" dia. circle; twist to secure. Glue 2" of stem to back of each mirror.

2. Glue two wings to back of each mirror.

3. Cut ribbon into six 18" lengths. Place two ribbons together and tie into a bow. Glue one bow to front of each mirror handle.

4. Glue three jewels to front of each mirror.

BIRTHDAY BEAR

*W*ish a little girl a "beary" special birthday with a very special bear! Our frilly angel bear is crowned with the honoree's birthstone and all decked out in her best outfit — made from inexpensive lace doilies — to bring a smile to the day's celebrity.

WHAT TO BUY

11"h stuffed bear with movable arms and legs, 7^1/$_2$" x 11^1/$_2$" oval doily, 9^1/$_2$" dia. round doily, 4" heart-shaped doily, one package of white feathers, an 18mm heart-shaped acrylic jewel (refer to birthstone key, pg. 118), and ^{1}/$_4$"w satin ribbon to match jewel (10-yd. spool)

THINGS YOU HAVE AT HOME

White embroidery floss, embroidery needle, scrap of poster board, polyester fiberfill, and a hot glue gun

ANGEL BIRTHDAY BEAR

1. For apron skirt, fold oval doily in half lengthwise. Use three strands of floss to baste ^{1}/$_8$" from folded edge. Pull floss to gather skirt to measure 5^1/$_2$" wide; knot and trim floss ends.

2. For apron bib, overlap gathered edge of skirt 2" over right side of heart-shaped doily; glue in place.

3. Cut one 34" and two 22" lengths of ribbon. Center 34" ribbon length over gathers of apron; glue in place. Glue one end of each 22" ribbon length to top wrong side of apron bib. Cut an 8" length of ribbon; tie into a bow and glue in place over center of apron.

4. For hat, use three strands of floss to baste around remaining doily, 2" from edge. Pull floss to gather hat to fit head; knot and trim floss ends.

5. Cut a 12" length of ribbon; tie into a bow. Glue bow to front of hat.

6. Glue jewel over knot of bow.

7. For wings, cut a 2" x 4" rectangle from poster board. Covering both sides and pointing feathers in opposite directions, glue feathers onto poster board rectangle.

8. Place apron on bear; tie waist ribbon into bow at bear's back. Centering wings on back of bear, bring bib ribbons over shoulders, crossing over wings; bring up around front of arms and tie into a bow at back of neck.

BARRETTE BEAUTY

*Y*our favorite little girl will never have to worry about losing her hair barrettes again — this beauty will "hang on" to them for her! The long yarn braids provide room for lots of barrettes, and the whimsical organizer also makes a colorful accent for a bedroom door or wall.

WHAT TO BUY
8" x 10" x ¼" sheet of foam core board, flesh-colored paint, dark orange yarn, ¼ yd. of 2"w gathered eyelet lace, 1 yd. of 1"w green ribbon, ⅜ yd. of ⅞"w pink pin-dot ribbon, ½ yd. of ¾"w blue ribbon, ½ yd. of 1"w purple ribbon, stem of artificial daisies, large straw doll hat, hair barrettes, and green chenille stems

THINGS YOU HAVE AT HOME
Drawing compass, craft knife, paintbrush, brown and black felt-tip markers, pink colored pencil, two rubber bands, four bobby pins, floral wire, and a hot glue gun

BARRETTE BEAUTY
1. For head, use drawing compass to draw an 8" dia. circle on foam core board. Use craft knife to cut out circle.

88   *(Continued on page 95)*

FLOWERS FOR MOM

*K*ids will have a great time creating this cute pillow for Mom! Simple stitches make it easy for young ones to attach colorful shapes to the soft felt pillow. The project is a fun way to get children involved in crafting, and it costs less than $4 to make.

WHAT TO BUY
Yellow, pink, light blue, red, purple, and green felt pieces; two blue felt pieces; yellow and red embroidery floss; and polyester fiberfill

THINGS YOU HAVE AT HOME
Tracing paper, embroidery needle, and assorted buttons

FLOWER AND HEART PILLOW
1. Trace flower, leaf, and heart patterns (pg. 120) onto tracing paper; cut out.

Use patterns to cut eleven flowers, ten leaves, and eleven hearts from felt pieces.

2. Leaving an opening for stuffing, use six strands of red floss to sew blue felt pieces together. Stuff pillow with fiberfill; sew opening closed.

3. Referring to *Embroidery Stitches* (pg. 125), use six strands of yellow floss and Cross Stitches to sew hearts and flowers to one side of pillow. Use Running Stitch to sew leaves in place.

4. Sew buttons to flower centers and hearts as desired.

FRIENDSHIP PILLOWCASE

*G*ive fun-loving youngsters a clever way to hold on to those exciting slumber party memories! For an inexpensive keepsake, each child can draw a face and other designs onto a pillowcase using fabric crayons. They can then autograph each other's cases and add ribbon bows for a cute final touch.

WHAT TO BUY
White pillowcase, fabric crayons, and $^1/_2$ yd. of $^3/_8$"w ribbon

THINGS YOU HAVE AT HOME
Safety pin

FRIENDSHIP PILLOWCASE

1. Following crayon manufacturer's instructions, have child draw face and desired designs on pillowcase.

2. Brush excess color flecks from pillowcase.

3. Tie ribbon into a bow; pin to pillowcase.

LET'S PRETEND

Little girls love the world of make-believe, and this fun dress-up kit will provide hours of pretend play. The kit has everything a young miss needs to look like a princess, including sparkling jewelry, a feathered fan, and a tiara. Pack it all in a big gift bag for a fun playtime treat!

WHAT TO BUY

$1/2$ yd. of pink taffeta, 1 yd. of $5/8$"w pink satin ribbon, small faux pearls (5-yd. package), 18mm round acrylic jewels, package of white feathers, white visor, one pair of clip-on earrings, one pair of play shoes, and a large pink gift bag

THINGS YOU HAVE AT HOME

Tracing paper, poster board, thread, jumbo craft stick, and a hot glue gun

DRESS-UP KIT

Use $1/4$"w seam allowance for all sewing unless otherwise indicated. Referring to Making Patterns (pg. 123), trace tiara, purse, purse flap, and fan patterns (pg. 122) onto tracing paper; cut out.

Purse

1. Use purse and purse flap patterns to cut two of each shape from fabric.

2. Matching right sides and leaving an opening for turning, sew purse together. Turn right side out; press. Sew opening closed. Tuck sewn end into finished end to make a pocket.

3. Matching right sides, sew along short edges of flap. Turn right side out; press. Press raw edges of flap $1/4$" to wrong side. Topstitch long edge of flap along back edge of purse. For handle, press each end of ribbon $1/4$" to wrong side. Sew ends to back of flap.

4. Cut an $8^{3}/4$" length of pearls; glue along point of flap. Glue one jewel to center of flap.

Fan

1. Use fan pattern to cut two pieces from poster board. Cutting $1/2$" outside edges, use pattern to cut one shape from fabric. Center one poster board piece on wrong side of fabric piece. Overlap and glue edges of fabric to back of poster board.

2. Cut a $9^{3}/4$" length of pearls; glue around edge of fan. Glue one jewel to center of fan. Glue one end of craft stick to back of fan. Arrange and glue feathers
(Continued on page 95)

PUZZLE PALS

*T*his quick project will help youngsters connect! Kids will have tons of fun fashioning jazzy sets of pins using puzzle pieces, dimensional paint, ribbons, and assorted buttons. The fun jewelry will make snazzy party favors, too!

WHAT TO BUY
Child's puzzle with large pieces, white dimensional paint, ⅛"w ribbon (10-yd. spool), and pin backs (4-pack)

THINGS YOU HAVE AT HOME
Spray acrylic sealer, assorted buttons, and a hot glue gun

PUZZLE PAL PINS
1. Spray each of two interlocking puzzle pieces with acrylic sealer; allow to dry.

2. Referring to *Painting Basics* (pg. 123), use paint to write "BEST" on one puzzle piece and "FRIENDS" on remaining puzzle piece; allow to dry.

3. Glue desired buttons onto each puzzle piece.

4. Cut two 6" lengths of ribbon; tie each length into a bow. Glue one bow to each puzzle piece.

5. Glue a pin back to each puzzle piece.

TURTLE TIME

*K*ids can help make this adorable turtle pillow for a playtime pal! Created from economical felt and stuffed with fiberfill, the comical creature is a comfy partner for watching television or napping on long car trips.

WHAT TO BUY

$1/2$ yd. of green felt, $1/4$ yd. of yellow felt, two black felt pieces, polyester fiberfill, black embroidery floss, and two 23mm wiggle eyes

THINGS YOU HAVE AT HOME

String, pencil, thumbtack, drawing compass, tracing paper, pinking shears, thread, embroidery needle, and craft glue

TURTLE PILLOW

Use $1/4$"w seam allowance for all sewing unless otherwise indicated.

1. For turtle shell top and bottom, cut two 18" squares from green felt. Follow *Cutting a Fabric Circle* (pg. 127) and use pinking shears to cut one 17" dia. circle from each square.

(Continued on page 95)

93

PERKY PUPPETS

UNDER $5!

These perky puppets can carry youngsters into a world of creative playtime. The cuddly no-sew characters assemble quickly using felt and glue. For about a quarter apiece, you can keep little neighbors, friends, and relatives entertained for hours!

WHAT TO BUY
Ecru, yellow, pink, orange, tan, and brown felt pieces; 5mm wiggle eyes; and yellow feathers (¹/₂-oz. bag)

THINGS YOU HAVE AT HOME
Tracing paper, brown marker, and craft glue

FINGER PUPPETS
Duck
1. Trace dog body, puppet back, duck bill, and wing patterns (pg. 121) onto tracing paper; cut out. Use patterns to cut body, wing, and puppet back from yellow felt. Cut duck bill from orange felt.

2. Glue one feather to wrong side of head. Fold duck bill on fold line; use a dab of glue to secure. Arrange eyes, bill, and wings on front of duck; glue in place.

3. Fold puppet back at each fold line. Matching wrong sides, glue puppet back to body.

4. Glue a tail feather to back of puppet.

Dog
1. Trace dog body, ear, nose, tail, puppet back, and tummy patterns (pg. 121) onto tracing paper; cut out. Use patterns to cut body and puppet back from tan felt. Cut two ears, one nose, and one tail from brown felt. Cut tummy from ecru felt.

2. Arrange tummy, nose, eyes, and ears on front of body; glue in place. Use brown marker to draw face and paw prints.

3. Fold puppet back at each fold line. Matching wrong sides, glue puppet back to body.

4. Glue tail to back of puppet.

(Continued on page 95)

94

BARRETTE BEAUTY
(Continued from page 88)

2. For face, paint one side of circle; allow to dry.

3. Use markers to draw details on face. Use pencil to add color to cheeks.

4. For braid, cut thirty 38" lengths of yarn. Matching ends, bundle lengths together. Knot a 6" length of yarn around bundle at one end. Dividing into three groups of ten, braid bundle to within 2" from end. Wrap a rubber band around end of braid to secure. Cut a 4" length of 1"w green ribbon; tie into a knot around rubber band. Remove one daisy from stem; glue over knot of ribbon.

5. Repeat Step 4 for remaining braid. Arrange braids on face; glue in place.

6. For bangs, cut thirty 5" lengths of yarn. Leaving 4" free, glue yarn lengths side by side along top of face.

7. For collar, turn ends of lace under 1/2"; glue in place. Glue hemmed edge of lace onto back of face below chin. Tie pink ribbon into a bow; glue over center of collar.

8. Cut straw hat in half. Slightly covering bangs, glue one half of hat to top of head. For hatband, cut a 10" length of 1"w green ribbon; glue to hat, overlapping ends to back. Remove three daisies and one leaf from stem. Cut a 7" length of chenille stem; fold in half, twisting at fold. Glue a daisy to each end of chenille stem. Glue fold of chenille stem to hatband. Glue remaining daisy and leaf over chenille stem on hatband.

9. Cut blue and purple ribbon lengths in half; tie each half into a bow. Slide a bobby pin through knot in back of each bow; pin bows to braids.

10. For hanger, cut a 3" piece of floral wire; bend into a loop. Glue hanger to back of head.

11. Clip barrettes to braids.

DRESS-UP KIT
(Continued from page 91)

on back of fan. Glue remaining poster board piece over feathers on back of fan.

Tiara

1. Use tiara pattern to cut one shape from poster board. Cutting 1/2" outside edges, use pattern to cut one shape from fabric. Center poster board shape on wrong side of fabric shape. Overlapping outside edge and ends of tiara 1/2" and clipping curves as necessary, glue outside edges to wrong side of poster board shape. Glue ends of feathers to wrong side of tiara. Overlapping remaining raw edge of fabric 1/2" over top edge of visor, glue tiara onto visor.

2. Cut one 13" and one 16" length of pearls; glue along edges of tiara. Glue one jewel to center of tiara.

Earrings

1. For each earring, glue two feathers to back of one jewel.

2. Glue jewel to front of earring clip.

Shoes

1. For each shoe cover, cut a 6" x 12" rectangle of fabric. Matching wrong sides, glue long edges together to form a tube; turn right side out. Turn ends of tube 1/4" to wrong side.

2. Glue one end of tube to each bottom edge of strap. Twist center of shoe cover to form a knot; glue to strap. Glue edges of cover over edges of strap. Glue feathers to knot.

Necklace

1. Cut one 26", one 30", and one 34" length of pearls.

2. Glue ends of strands to back of one jewel.

Bag

1. Write "Dress Up" on front of gift bag; glue pearls along drawn lines.

2. Glue three feathers onto back of each of two jewels. Glue jewels to front of bag.

TURTLE PILLOW
(Continued from page 93)

2. Use drawing compass to draw 3 1/2" dia. and 2 1/2" dia. circle patterns onto tracing paper; cut out. Use pinking shears and 3 1/2" pattern to cut ten circles from black felt and 2 1/2" pattern to cut ten circles from yellow felt.

3. Centering yellow circles on black circles, sew circles onto turtle shell top.

4. Trace turtle head, tail, and foot patterns (pg. 100) onto tracing paper; cut out. Use pinking shears and patterns to cut two tails, two heads, and eight feet from yellow felt.

5. Leaving straight edges open for stuffing, machine stitch each pair of foot pieces, head pieces, and tail pieces together. Stuff each pair lightly with fiberfill; sew openings closed. Arrange feet, tail, and head on turtle shell bottom; sew in place.

6. Leaving an opening for stuffing, sew turtle shell top to turtle shell bottom. Stuff with fiberfill; sew opening closed.

7. Use twelve strands of floss to make two 1" long straight stitches on each foot for toes.

8. Glue eyes to head.

FINGER PUPPETS
(Continued from page 94)

Bear

1. Trace bear body, ear, paw, muzzle, tummy, and puppet back patterns (pg. 120) onto tracing paper; cut out. Use patterns to cut bear body and puppet back from brown felt. Cut muzzle, tummy, and paws from tan felt. Cut two ears from pink felt.

2. Arrange eyes, ears, muzzle, paws, and tummy on front of body; glue in place.

3. Use marker to draw face on muzzle.

4. Fold puppet back at each fold line. Matching wrong sides, glue puppet back to body.

PATTERNS

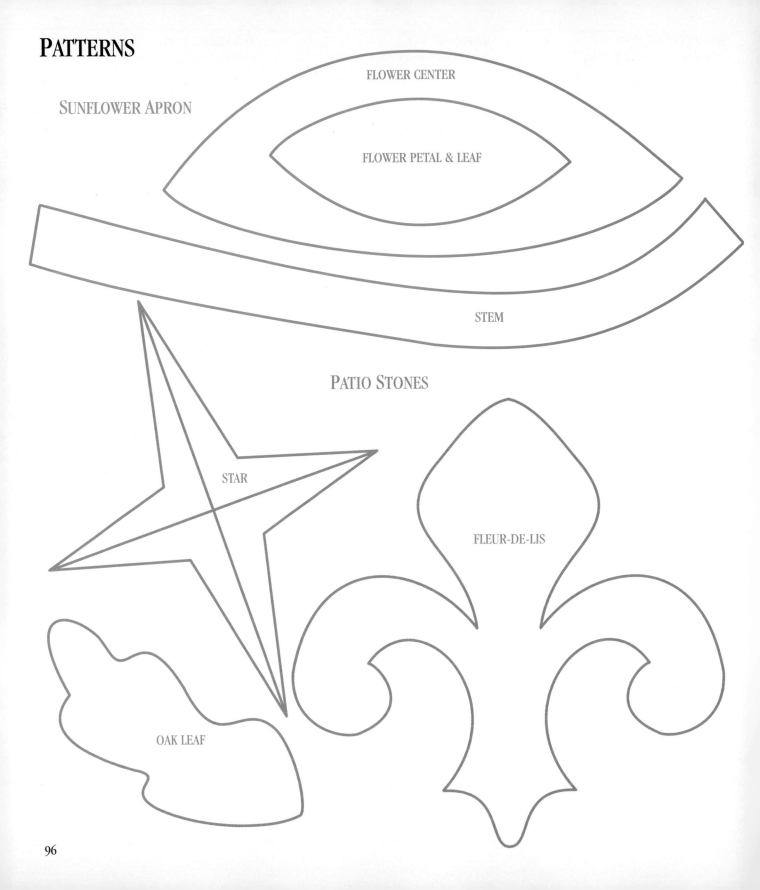

SUNFLOWER APRON

FLOWER CENTER

FLOWER PETAL & LEAF

STEM

PATIO STONES

STAR

FLEUR-DE-LIS

OAK LEAF

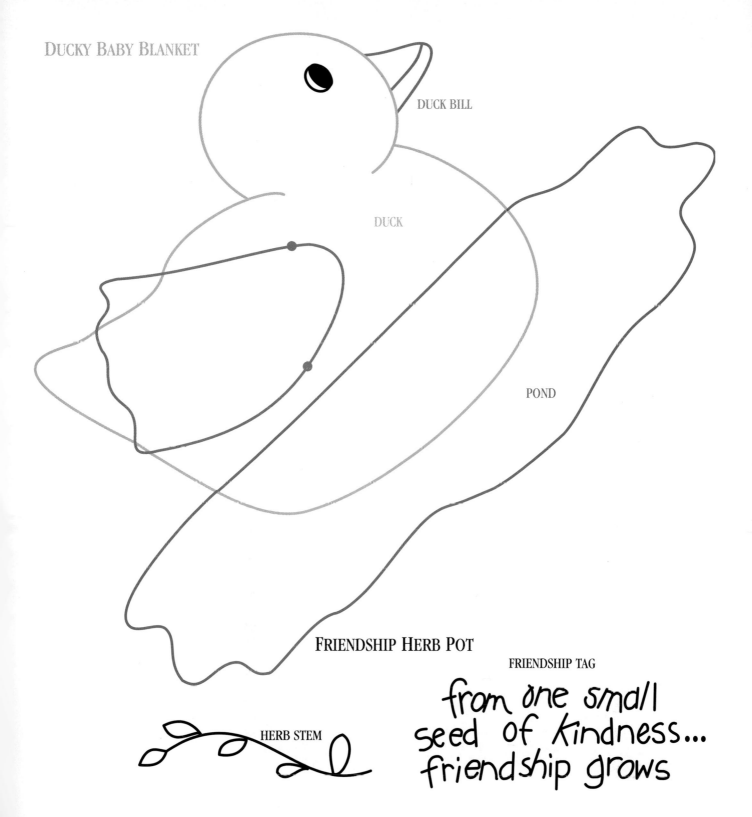

DUCKY BABY BLANKET

DUCK BILL

DUCK

POND

FRIENDSHIP HERB POT

FRIENDSHIP TAG

HERB STEM

from one small
seed of kindness...
friendship grows

PATTERNS (continued)

FRIENDSHIP WREATH

X	DMC	¼X	B'ST	COLOR
▲	797		╱	dk blue
◐	799		╱	blue
◇	800		╱	lt blue
•	797			French Knot

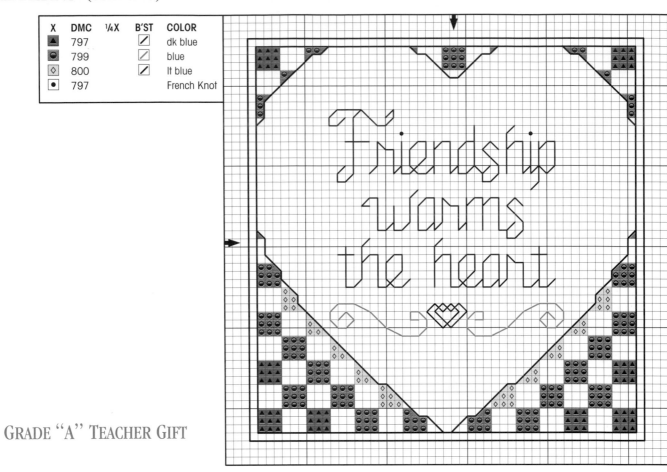

GRADE "A" TEACHER GIFT

WORM

CROSS-STITCHED MINI TOTE

X	DMC	B'ST
•	blanc	
	309	╱
◆	422	
★	838	╱
✳	839	
•	309	French Knot

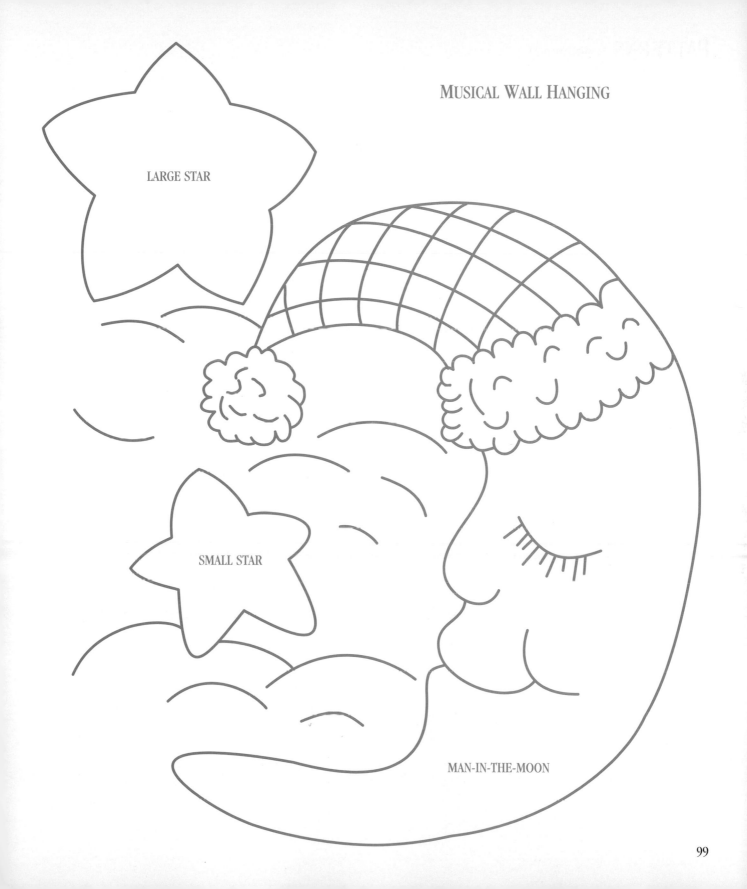

LARGE STAR

MUSICAL WALL HANGING

SMALL STAR

MAN-IN-THE-MOON

99

PATTERNS (continued)

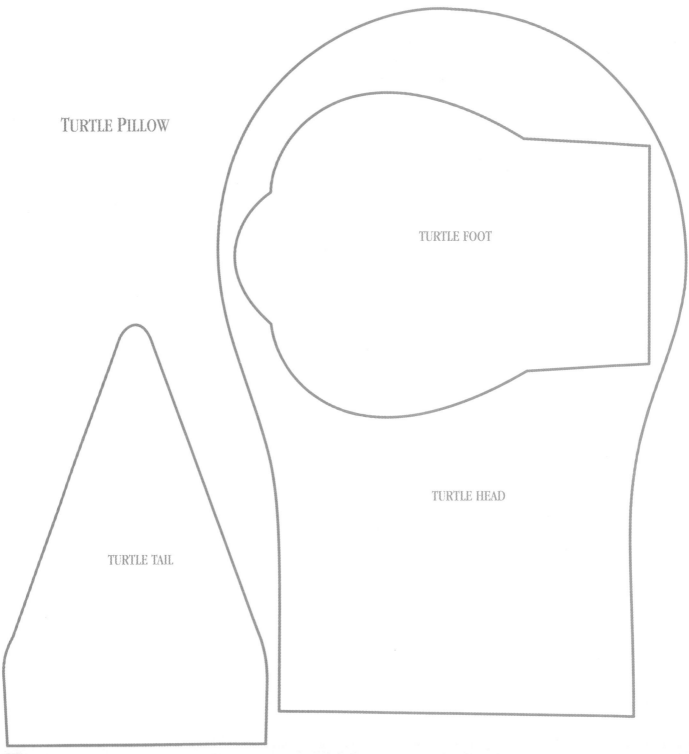

TURTLE PILLOW

TURTLE FOOT

TURTLE HEAD

TURTLE TAIL

CROSS-STITCHED
BABY SWEATSHIRT

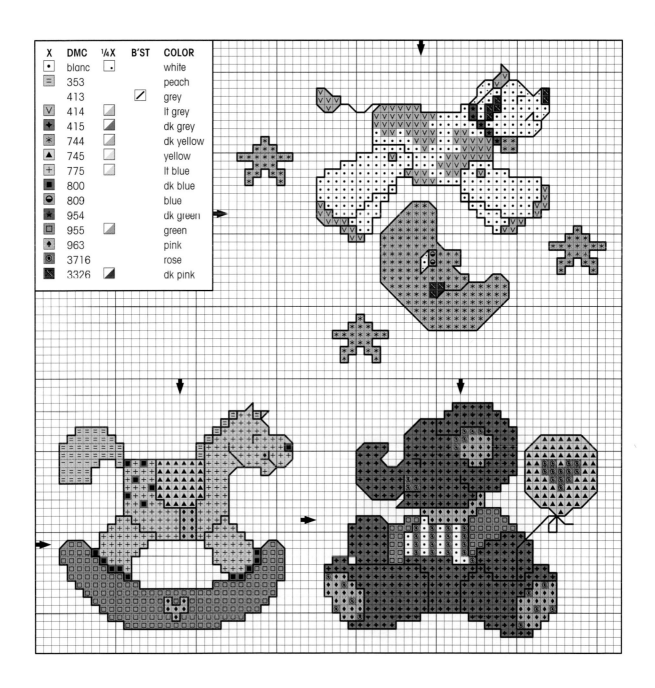

X	DMC	¼X	B'ST	COLOR
•	blanc	•		white
=	353			peach
	413		/	grey
V	414			lt grey
✦	415			dk grey
✳	744			dk yellow
▲	745			yellow
+	775			lt blue
■	800			dk blue
◒	809			blue
★	954			dk green
▢	955			green
◆	963			pink
◉	3716			rose
▨	3326			dk pink

FRIENDSHIP LAVENDER
PILLOW

ST. PATRICK'S DAY WREATH

SHAMROCK

VALENTINE FLOWERPOT

HEART

Tea-Towel Tote

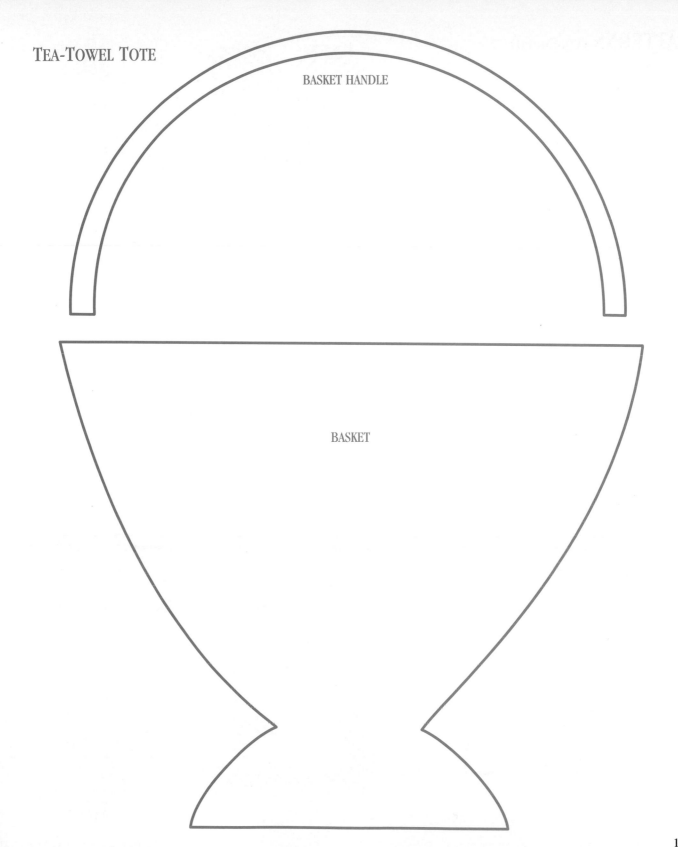

BASKET HANDLE

BASKET

PATTERNS (continued)

PLASTIC CANVAS BOOKMARKS

COLOR KEY

- ✎ purple
- ✎ dk pink
- ✎ pink
- ✎ green
- ✎ yellow
- ● purple French Knot

MOOSE TREAT CONTAINER

MOOSE

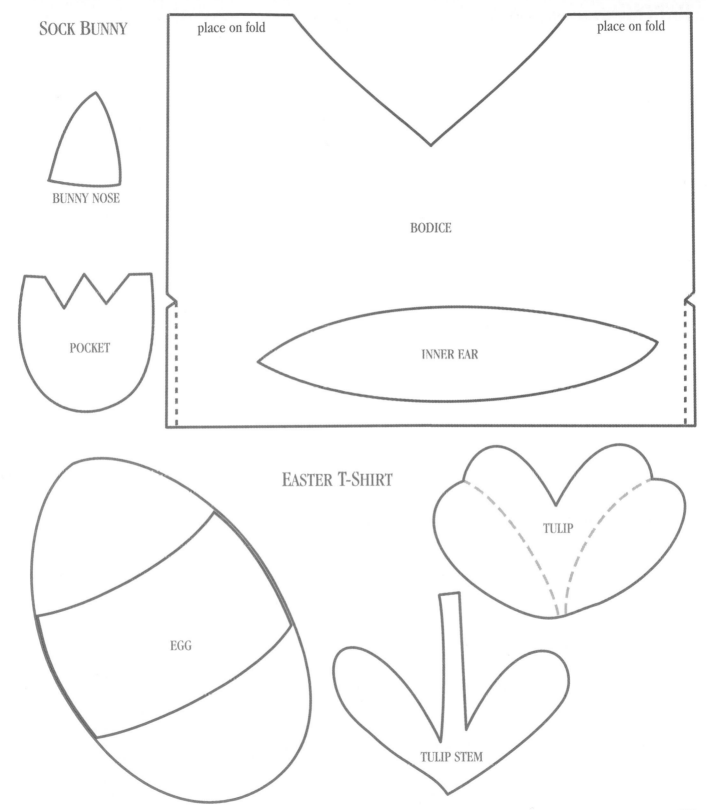

SOCK BUNNY

BUNNY NOSE

place on fold   place on fold

BODICE

POCKET

INNER EAR

EASTER T-SHIRT

EGG

TULIP

TULIP STEM

PATTERNS (continued)

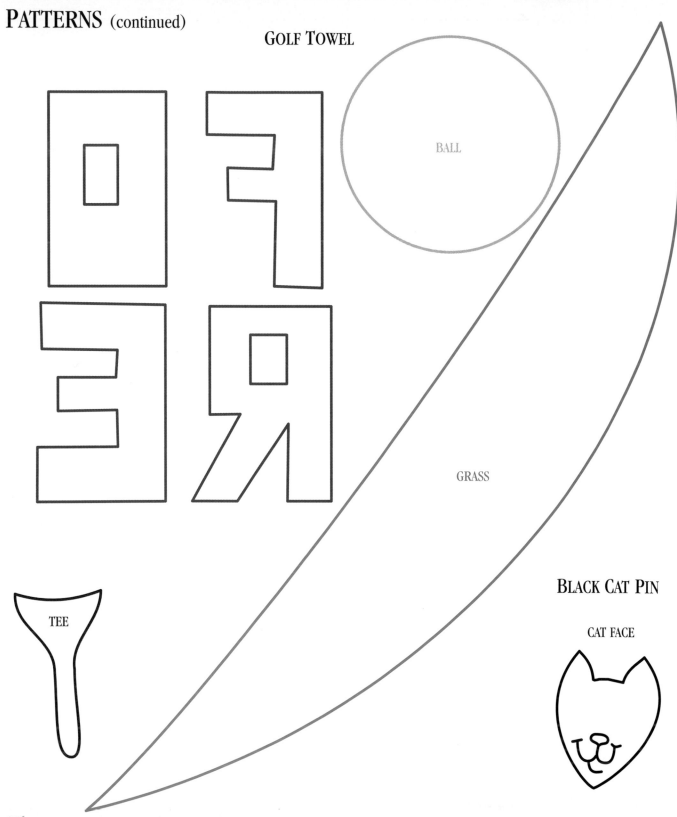

GOLF TOWEL

BALL

GRASS

TEE

BLACK CAT PIN

CAT FACE

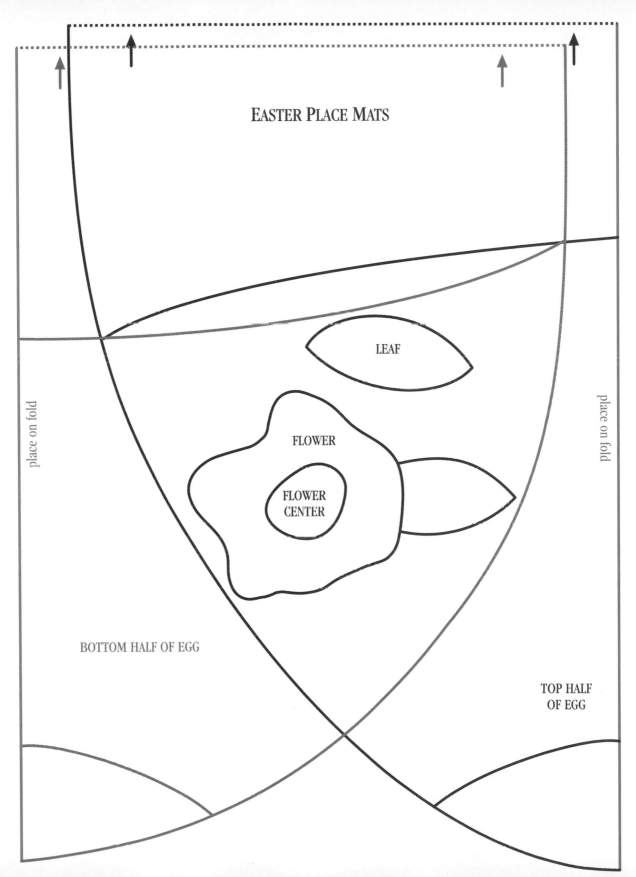

EASTER PLACE MATS

LEAF

place on fold

place on fold

FLOWER

FLOWER
CENTER

BOTTOM HALF OF EGG

TOP HALF
OF EGG

107

**UNCLE SAM
ORNAMENTS**

UNCLE SAM

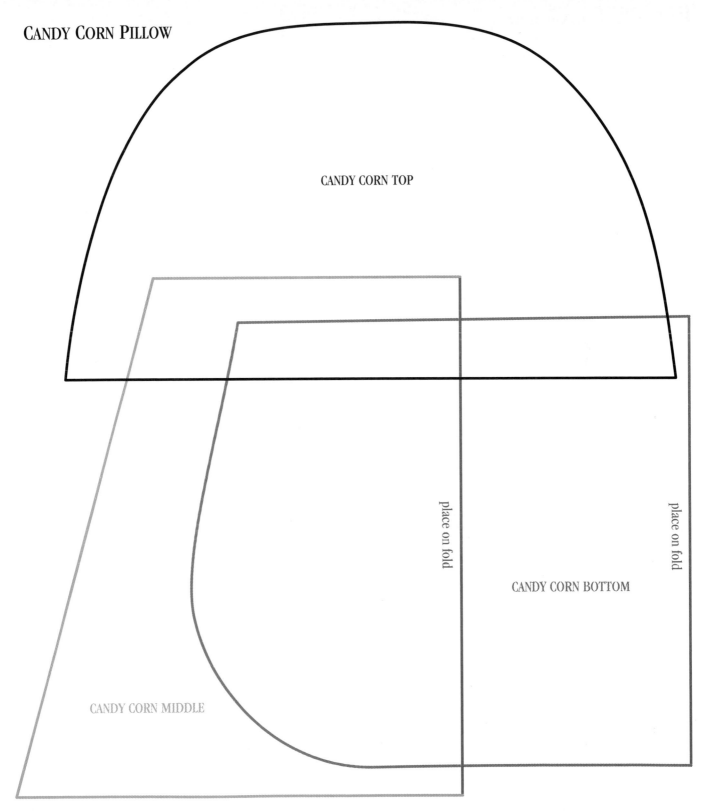

CANDY CORN PILLOW

CANDY CORN TOP

place on fold

place on fold

CANDY CORN BOTTOM

CANDY CORN MIDDLE

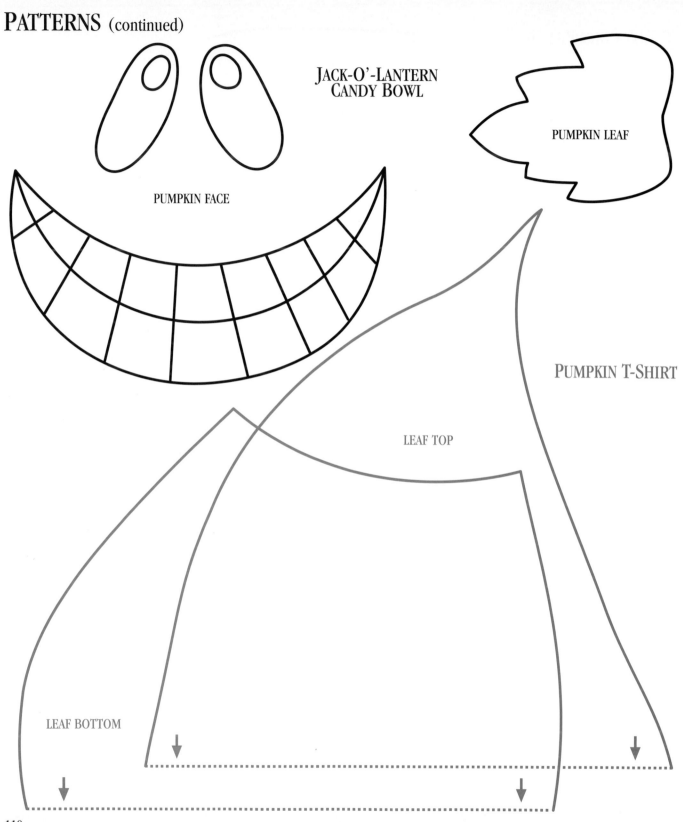

JACK-O'-LANTERN
CANDY BOWL

PUMPKIN LEAF

PUMPKIN FACE

PUMPKIN T-SHIRT

LEAF TOP

LEAF BOTTOM

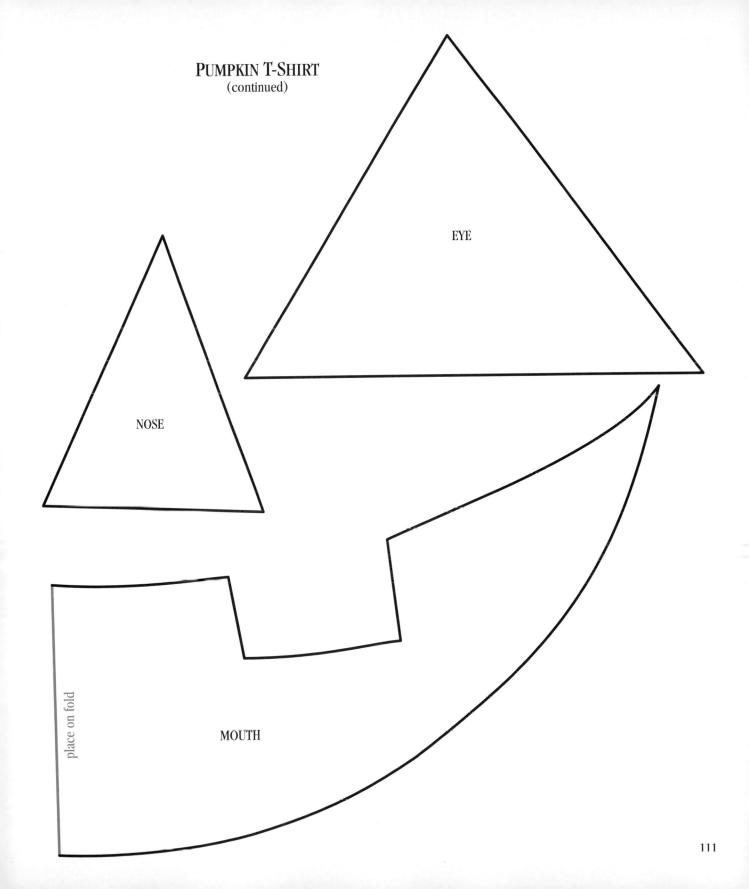

EYE

NOSE

place on fold

MOUTH

PATTERNS (continued)

CROSS-STITCHED PUMPKINS

X	DMC	1/4X	B'ST	COLOR
•	blanc	•		white
▲	310		/	black
◕	434			brown
◆	701			green
✳	703			lt green
★	725			dk yellow
=	894			pink
■	947			orange
▣	970			lt orange

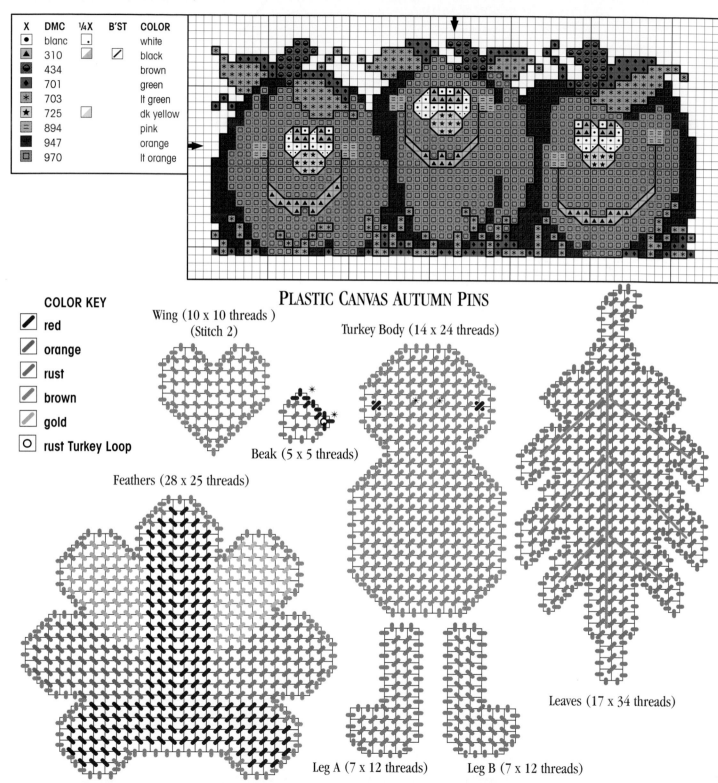

PLASTIC CANVAS AUTUMN PINS

COLOR KEY
- / red
- / orange
- / rust
- / brown
- / gold
- ○ rust Turkey Loop

Wing (10 x 10 threads)
(Stitch 2)

Beak (5 x 5 threads)

Turkey Body (14 x 24 threads)

Leaves (17 x 34 threads)

Feathers (28 x 25 threads)

Leg A (7 x 12 threads)   Leg B (7 x 12 threads)

TURKEY BOWL

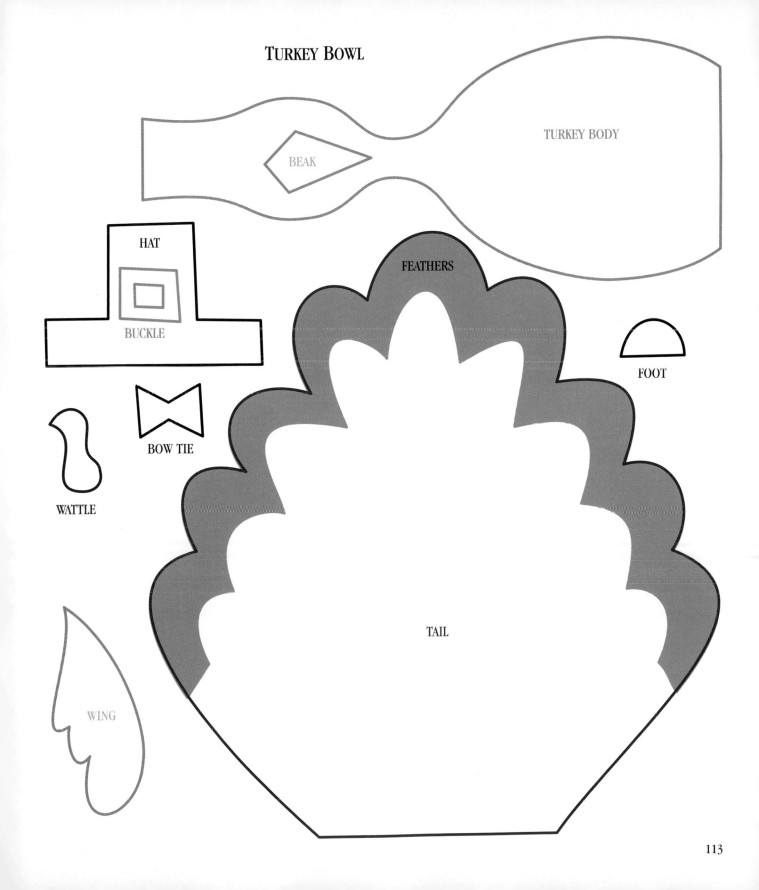

TURKEY BODY

BEAK

HAT

BUCKLE

FEATHERS

FOOT

BOW TIE

WATTLE

TAIL

WING

113

PATTERNS (continued)

Christmas Sweatshirt

STAR

HORSE

TREE

GINGERBREAD MAN

OVAL FRAME

STAR

SANTA

TREE

LETTERS

Y

UTRPONEB

PAPER SANTA ORNAMENTS

PAPER SANTA

SNOWMAN CANDY JAR

SNOWMAN NOSE

HAT

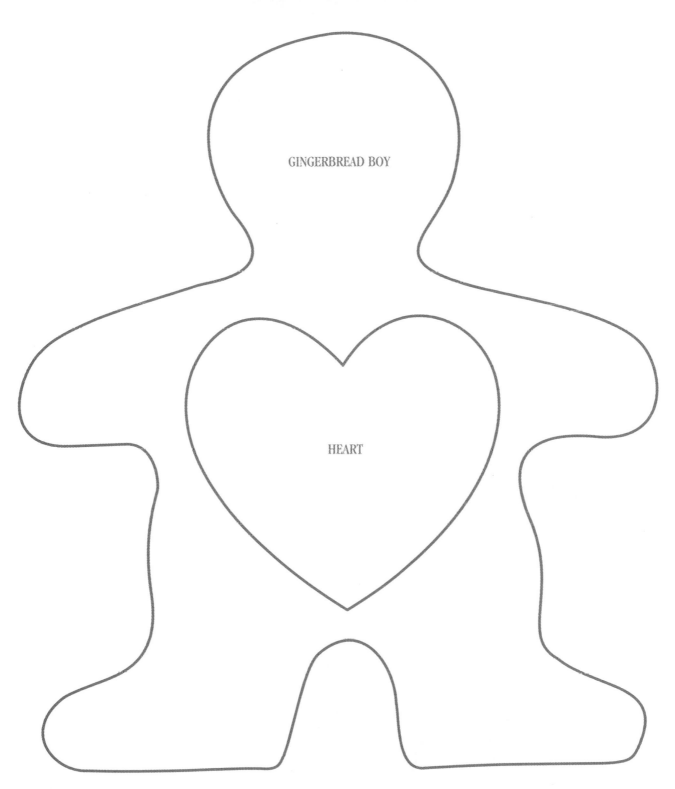

GINGERBREAD BOY

HEART

PATTERNS (continued)

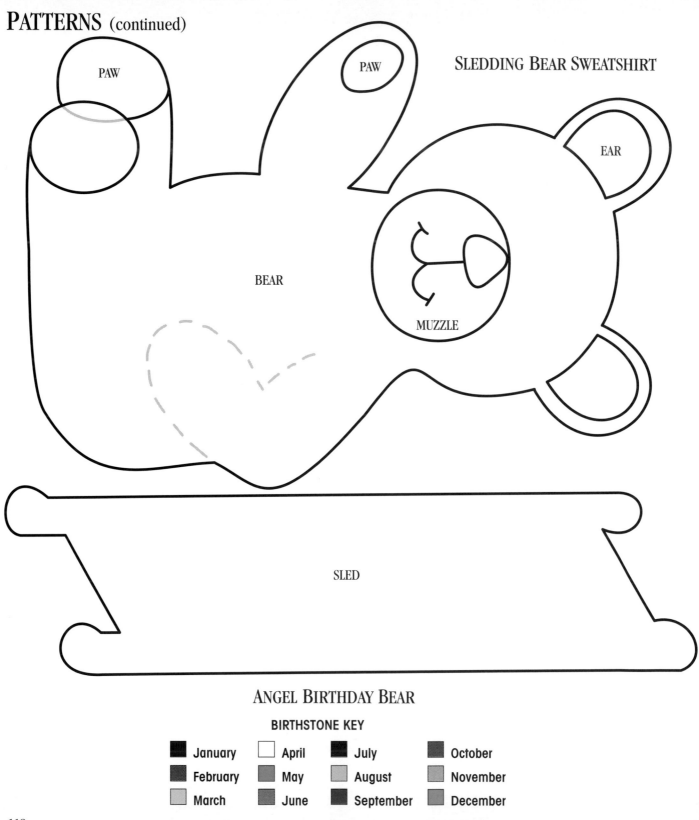

PAW

PAW

SLEDDING BEAR SWEATSHIRT

EAR

BEAR

MUZZLE

SLED

ANGEL BIRTHDAY BEAR

BIRTHSTONE KEY

	January		April		July		October
	February		May		August		November
	March		June		September		December

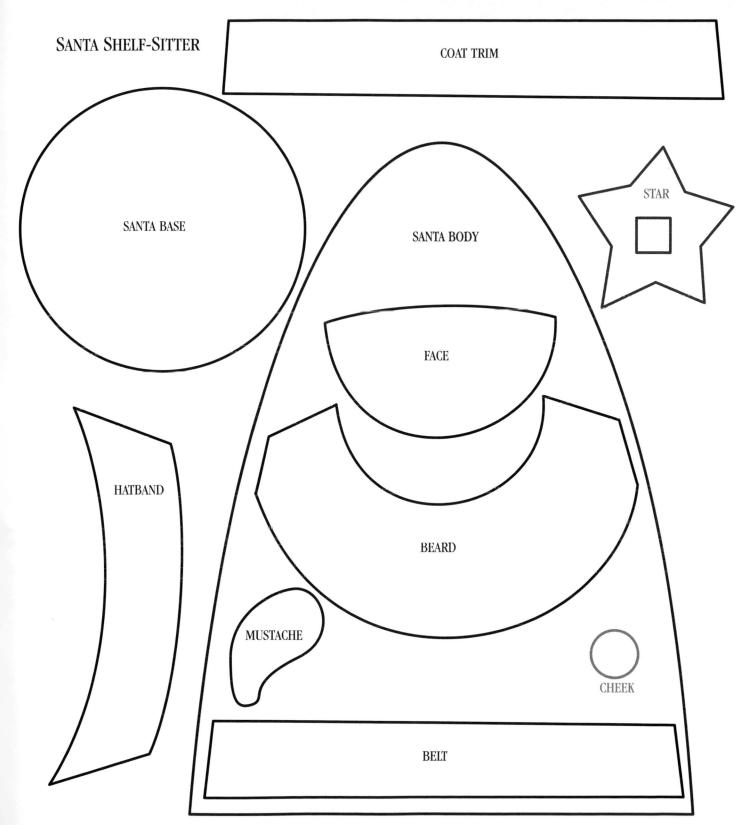

SANTA SHELF-SITTER

COAT TRIM

SANTA BASE

STAR

SANTA BODY

FACE

HATBAND

BEARD

MUSTACHE

CHEEK

BELT

PATTERNS (continued)

PET'S ELF COSTUME

COLLAR

place on fold

FINGER PUPPETS

EAR

MUZZLE

FLOWER AND HEART PILLOW

BEAR BODY

PAW

HEART

FLOWER
CENTER

TUMMY

LEAF

FLOWER

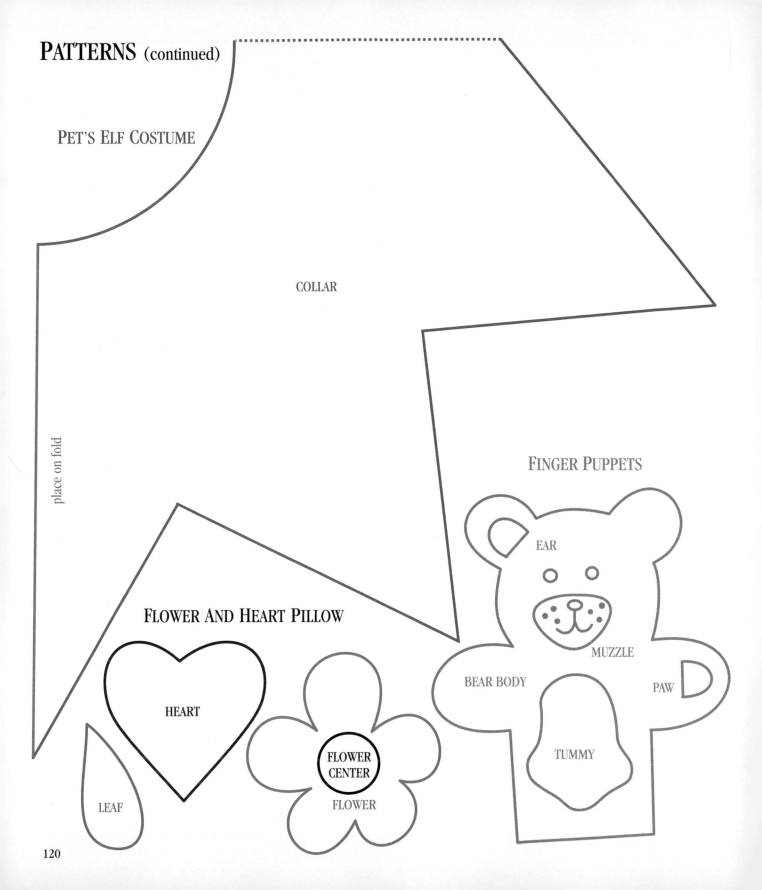

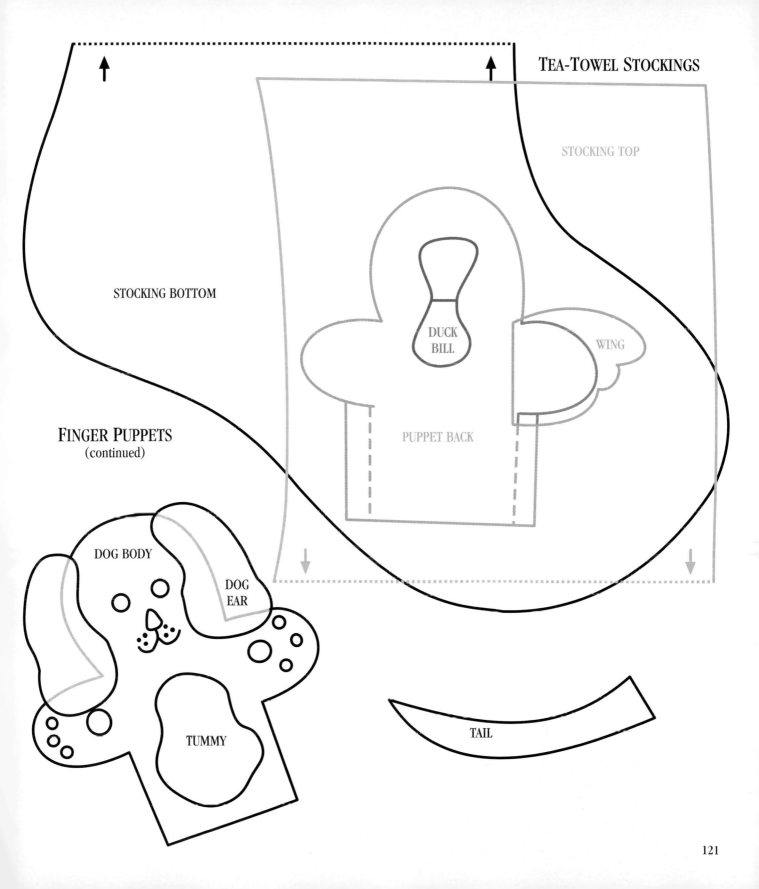

TEA-TOWEL STOCKINGS

STOCKING TOP

STOCKING BOTTOM

DUCK
BILL

WING

PUPPET BACK

FINGER PUPPETS
(continued)

DOG BODY

DOG
EAR

TUMMY

TAIL

121

DRESS-UP KIT

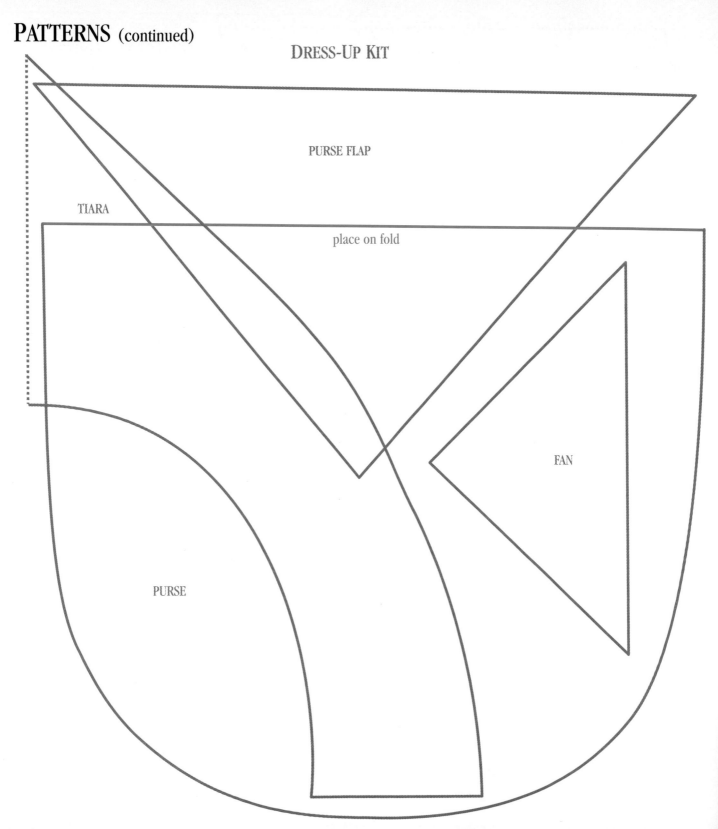

PURSE FLAP

TIARA

place on fold

FAN

PURSE

GENERAL INSTRUCTIONS

MAKING PATTERNS

Blue line on pattern indicates where traced pattern is to be placed on fold of material.

When patterns are stacked or overlapped, place tracing paper over pattern and follow a single colored line to trace pattern. Repeat to trace each pattern separately onto tracing paper.

For a more durable pattern, use translucent vinyl template material instead of tracing paper.

Half-patterns: Fold tracing paper in half. Place fold along dotted line and trace pattern half; turn folded paper over and draw over traced lines on remaining side. Unfold pattern; cut out.

Two-part patterns: Trace one part of pattern onto tracing paper. Match dotted line and arrows of traced part with dotted line and arrows of second part in book and trace second part; cut out.

Transferring a pattern: Make a tracing paper pattern. Position pattern on project. Place transfer paper coated side down between pattern and project. Use a stylus to trace over lines of patterns.

FUSING BASICS

To protect your ironing board, cover with muslin. Web material that sticks to iron may be removed with hot iron cleaner, available at fabric and craft stores.

Using fusible web: Place web side of paper-backed fusible web on wrong side of fabric. Follow manufacturer's instructions to fuse web to fabric. Remove paper backing. Position fused fabric web side down on project and press with heated iron for ten seconds. Repeat, lifting and repositioning iron until all fabric is fused.

Making fusible fabric appliqués: To prevent darker fabrics from showing through, white or light-colored fabrics may need to be lined with fusible interfacing before being fused.

Trace appliqué pattern onto paper side of web. When making more than one appliqué, leave at least 1" between shapes. Cutting 1/2" outside drawn shape, cut out web shape. Fuse to wrong side of fabric. Cut out shape along drawn lines. Remove paper backing. If pattern is a half-pattern or to make a reversed appliqué, make a tracing paper pattern (turn traced pattern over for reversed appliqué) and follow instructions using traced pattern.

STITCHED APPLIQUÉS

Stitching appliqués: Place paper or stabilizer on wrong side of background fabric under fused appliqué.

Beginning on a straight edge of appliqué if possible, position project under presser foot so that most of stitching will be on appliqué. Take a stitch in fabric and bring bobbin thread to top. Hold both threads toward you and sew over them for several stitches to secure. Stitch over all exposed raw edges of appliqué(s) and along detail lines as indicated in instructions.

When stitching is complete, remove stabilizer. Clip threads close to stitching.

PAINTING BASICS

Painting with a sponge shape: Cut out sponge shape according to project

instructions; dampen with water. Dip one side of sponge into paint and remove excess on a paper towel. Lightly press sponge shape on project, then carefully lift. Reapplying paint to sponge as necessary, repeat to paint additional shapes on project.

Stenciling: For stencil, cut a piece of template material at least 1" larger on all sides than pattern. Place template material directly over pattern in book. Use a pen to trace pattern onto template material. Place template material on cutting mat and use craft knife to cut out stencil sections, making sure edges are smooth.

Pour a small amount of paint onto a paper plate. Hold or tape (using removable tape) stencil in place on project. Dip a stencil brush or sponge piece in paint and remove excess on a paper towel. Brush or sponge should be almost dry to produce good results. Beginning at edge of cut-out area, apply paint in a stamping motion over stencil. Carefully remove stencil from project. To stencil a design in reverse, clean stencil and turn stencil over.

Painting with dimensional paint: Turn bottle upside down to fill tip before each use. While painting, clean tip often with a paper towel. If tip becomes clogged, insert a straight pin into opening to unclog.

To paint, touch tip to project. Squeezing and moving bottle steadily, apply paint to project, being careful not to flatten paint line. If painting detail lines, center line of paint over transferred line on project or freehand details as desired.

To correct a mistake, use a paring knife to gently scrape excess paint from project before it dries. Carefully remove stain with non-acetone nail polish remover on a cotton swab. A mistake may also be camouflaged by incorporating it into the design.

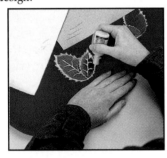

MULTI-LOOP BOW

Making a multi-loop bow: For first streamer, measure desired length of streamer from one end of ribbon and twist ribbon between fingers.

For first loop, keep right side of ribbon facing out and fold ribbon to front to form desired size loop; gather between fingers.

Fold ribbon to back to form another loop; gather between fingers. Continue to form loops, varying size as desired, until bow is desired size.

For remaining streamer, trim ribbon to desired length.

To secure bow, hold gathered loops tightly. Fold a length of floral wire around gathers of loops. Hold wire ends behind bow, gathering all loops forward; twist bow to tighten wire. Arrange loops and trim ribbon ends as desired.

CROSS STITCH

Preparing floss: If your project will be laundered, soak floss in a mixture of one cup water and one tablespoon vinegar for a few minutes and allow to dry before using to prevent colors from bleeding or fading.

Counted Cross Stitch (X): Work one Cross Stitch to correspond to each colored square in chart. For horizontal rows, work stitches in two journeys.

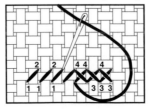

For vertical rows, complete each stitch as shown.

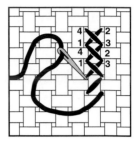

When working over 2 fabric threads, work Cross Stitch as shown.

Quarter Stitch (¼ X): Quarter Stitches are shown by triangular shapes of color in chart and color key.

Backstitch (B'ST): For outline detail, Backstitch (shown in chart and color key by black or colored straight lines) should be worked after all Cross Stitch has been completed.

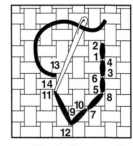

Working on Waste Canvas: Cut pieces of waste canvas and lightweight interfacing about 1" larger on all sides than finished design size. Center and pin interfacing to inside front of garment. Cover edges of canvas with masking tape. Find center of stitching area on canvas and mark with a pin. Find center of stitching area on garment and mark with a pin. Matching center of canvas to pin on garment, pin canvas in place. Stitching through all layers, baste along edges of canvas, from corner to corner, and from side to side. Mark center of canvas by using pink thread to baste down center. Beginning 1" from top of canvas, use a sharp needle to stitch design. Remove basting threads and trim canvas to about ¹/₂" from design. Use tweezers to pull out canvas threads one at a time. If necessary, slightly dampen canvas until it becomes soft enough to make removing threads easier.

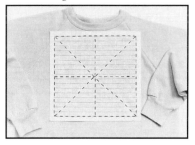

EMBROIDERY STITCHES

Preparing floss: If using embroidery floss for a project that will be laundered, soak floss in a mixture of one cup water and one tablespoon vinegar for a few minutes and allow to dry before using to prevent colors from bleeding or fading.

Straight Stitch: Referring to Fig. 1, come up at 1 and go down at 2.

Fig. 1

Running Stitch: Referring to Fig. 2, make a series of straight stitches with stitch length equal to the space between stitches.

Fig. 2

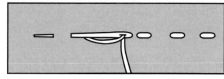

Cross Stitch: Referring to Fig. 3, bring needle up at 1; go down at 2. Bring needle up at 3; go down at 4. Repeat for each stitch.

Fig. 3

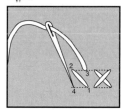

Blanket Stitch: Referring to Fig. 4, bring needle up at 1. Keeping thread below point of needle, go down at 2 and come up at 3. Continue working as shown (Fig. 5).

Fig. 4

Fig. 5

French Knot: Referring to Fig. 6, bring needle up at 1. Wrap floss once around needle and insert needle at 2, holding end of floss with non-stitching fingers. Tighten knot, then pull needle through fabric, holding floss until it must be released. For a larger knot, use more strands; wrap only once.

Fig. 6

Satin Stitch: Referring to Fig. 7, come up at odd numbers and go down at even numbers with the stitches touching but not overlapping.

Fig. 7

Stem Stitch: Referring to Fig. 8, come up at 1. Keeping the thread below the stitching line, go down at 2 and come up at 3. Go down at 4 and come up at 5.

Fig. 8

Lazy Daisy Stitch: Referring to Fig. 9, come up at 1 and make a counterclockwise loop with the thread. Go down at 1 and come up at 2, keeping the thread below point of needle. Secure loop by bringing thread over loop and going down at 2.

Fig. 9

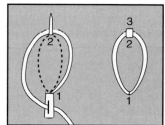

GENERAL INSTRUCTIONS (continued)

PLASTIC CANVAS

Gobelin Stitch: Referring to Fig. 1, work stitch over 2 or more threads or intersections. The number of threads or intersections may vary according to the chart.

Fig. 1

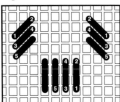

Backstitch: Referring to Fig. 2, work stitch over completed stitches to outline or define. It is sometimes worked over more than one thread. Backstitch may also be used to cover canvas.

Fig. 2

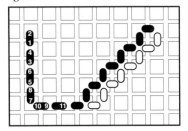

Cross Stitch: This stitch is composed of two stitches. The top of each cross must always be made in the same direction (refer to Fig. 3).

Fig. 3

French Knot: Referring to Fig. 4, bring needle up through hole; wrap yarn once around needle and insert needle in same hole, holding end of yarn with non-stitching fingers. Tighten knot, then pull needle through canvas, holding yarn until it must be released.

Fig. 4

Overcast Stitch: This stitch covers the edge of the plastic canvas and joins pieces of canvas. It may be necessary to go through the same hole more than once to get an even coverage on the edge, especially at the corners (refer to Fig. 5).

Fig. 5

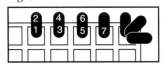

Tent Stitch: Referring to Fig. 6, work stitch in vertical or horizontal rows over one intersection.

Fig. 6

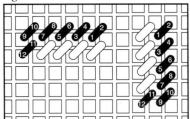

Turkey Loop Stitch: This stitch is composed of locked loops. Referring to Fig. 7, bring needle up through hole and back down through same hole, forming 1/2" loop on top of canvas. Locking Stitch is then made across thread directly above or to either side of loop.

Fig. 7

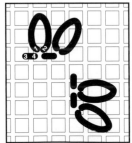

CROCHET

Abbreviations:

BLO	Back Loop(s) Only
ch	chain(s)
dc	double crochet(s)
FLO	Front Loop(s) Only
hdc	half double crochet(s)
Rnd(s)	Round(s)
sc	single crochet(s)
sp(s)	space(s)
st(s)	stitch(es)
tr	treble crochet(s)
YO	yarn over

★ — work instructions following ★ as many more times as indicated in addition to the first time.

( ) — work enclosed instructions as many times as specified by the number immediately following or work all enclosed instructions in the stitch or space indicated or contains explanatory remarks.

Gauge: Gauge is the number of stitches and rows or rounds per inch to make sure your project will be the right size. The hook size given in the instructions is only a guide. The project should never be made without first making a sample swatch about 4" square using the thread or yarn, hook, and stitch specified. Measure the swatch, counting stitches and rows carefully. If your swatch is smaller than what is specified in the instructions, try again with a larger hook; if it's larger, try again with a smaller one. Keep trying until you find the size hook that will give you the specified gauge.

Slip stitch (slip st): Insert hook in st or sp indicated, YO and draw through st and through loop on hook.

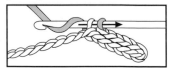

Single crochet (sc): Insert hook in st or sp indicated, YO and pull up a loop, YO and draw through both loops on hook.

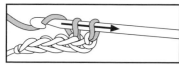

Half double crochet (hdc): YO, insert hook in st or sp indicated, YO and pull up a loop, YO and draw through all 3 loops on hook.

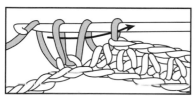

Double crochet (dc): YO, insert hook in st or sp indicated, YO and pull up a loop, YO and draw through two loops on hook (Fig. a), YO and draw though remaining two loops on hook (Fig. b).

Fig. a   Fig. b

 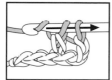

Treble crochet (tr): YO twice, insert hook in st or sp indicated, YO and pull up a loop (four loops on a hook, Fig. a), (YO and draw through two loops on hook) three times (Fig. b).

Fig. a   Fig. b

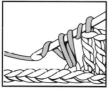 

Back or Front Loop Only (BLO, FLO): Work only in loop(s) indicated.

back   both   front

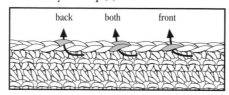

Free loops of a chain: When instructed to work in free loops of a chain, work in loop indicated by arrow.

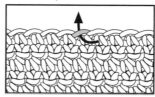

Reverse sc: Working from left to right, insert hook in st or sp to right of hook (Fig. a), YO and draw through, under and to left of loop on hook (two loops on hook, Fig. b), YO and draw through both loops on hook (Fig. c) (reverse sc made, Fig. d).

Fig. a   Fig. b

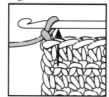 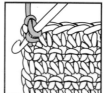

Fig. c   Fig. d

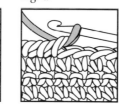

Back ridge: Work only in loop indicated by arrows.

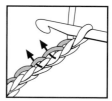

Joining with sc: When instructed to join with sc, begin with a slip knot on hook. Insert hook in st or sp indicated, YO and pull up a loop, YO and draw through both loops on hook.

CUTTING A FABRIC CIRCLE

Matching right sides, fold fabric square in half from top to bottom and in half again from left to right.

Refer to project instructions for diameter of fabric circle; determine radius of circle by dividing diameter in half. Tie one end of string to fabric marking pencil. Insert thumbtack through fabric as shown in Fig. 1 and mark cutting line. Cut along drawn line through all fabric layers. Unfold circle.

Fig. 1

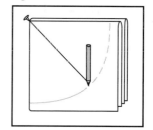

CREDITS

We want to extend a warm *thank you* to the generous people who allowed us to photograph our projects in their homes: Nancy Appleton, Ellison Madden, Peg Mills, Nancy and Duncan Porter, Penny Rudder, and Letitia Ryles.

To Magna IV Color Imaging of Little Rock, Arkansas, we say thank you for the superb color reproduction and excellent pre-press preparation.

We especially want to recognize photographers Mark Mathews, Larry Pennington, Karen Shirey, and Ken West of Peerless Photography, and Jerry R. Davis of Jerry Davis Photography, all of Little Rock, Arkansas, for their time, patience, and excellent work. We also wish to thank Sondra Daniel for her assistance as a photography stylist.

To the talented people who helped in the creation of the following projects in this book, we extend a special word of thanks:

- *Friendship Wreath*, page 19: Holly DeFount
- *Grade "A" Teacher's Gift*, page 23: Holly Witt
- *Eyeglass Cases*, page 26: Carolyn Pfeifer
- *Cross Stitch Baby Sweatshirt*, page 29: Linda Gillum
- *Cross Stitch Mini Tote*, page 30: Kooler Design Studio, Inc.
- *Sunflower Dish Towel*, page 32: Maggie Weldon
- *Pansy Coasters*, page 35: Dick Martin
- *Plastic Canvas Bookmarks*, page 38: Dick Martin
- *Crocheted Heart T-Shirt*, page 44: Linda Luder
- *Uncle Sam Ornament*, page 57: Susan Cousineau
- *Cross Stitch Pumpkins*, page 64: Terrie Lee Steinmeyer
- *Moose Treat Container*, page 65: Holly Witt
- *Plastic Canvas Autumn Pins*, page 67: Sandy and Honey for Studio M
- *Paper Santa Ornament*, pages 70-71: Susan Cousineau
- *Santa Shelf Sitter*, page 74: Holly Witt
- *Finger Puppets*, page 94: Kathy Wegner

Thanks also go to the people who assisted in making and testing projects in this book: Kandi Ashford, Beverly Garrett, Muriel Hicks, Connie McGaughey, and Lorissa Smith.